Certified Forensic Consultant Body of Knowledge

Center for National Threat Assessment

Certified Forensic Consultant Body of Knowledge
American College of Forensic Examiners Institute
ISBN: 978-1-4987-5207-7

The Certified Criminal Investigator Body of Knowledge
American College of Forensic Examiners Institute
ISBN: 978-1-4987-5205-3

Sensitive Security Information, Certified® (SSI) Body of Knowledge
American Board for Certification in Homeland Security
ISBN: 978-1-4987-5211-4

Certified Forensic Consultant Body of Knowledge

American College of
Forensic Examiners Institute

CRC Press is an imprint of the
Taylor & Francis Group, an **Informa** business

CRC Press
Taylor & Francis Group
6000 Broken Sound Parkway NW, Suite 300
Boca Raton, FL 33487-2742

© 2016 by American College of Forensic Examiners Institute
CRC Press is an imprint of Taylor & Francis Group, an Informa business

No claim to original U.S. Government works

Printed on acid-free paper
Version Date: 20151028

International Standard Book Number-13: 978-1-4987-5207-7 (Paperback)

This book contains information obtained from authentic and highly regarded sources. Reasonable efforts have been made to publish reliable data and information, but the author and publisher cannot assume responsibility for the validity of all materials or the consequences of their use. The authors and publishers have attempted to trace the copyright holders of all material reproduced in this publication and apologize to copyright holders if permission to publish in this form has not been obtained. If any copyright material has not been acknowledged please write and let us know so we may rectify in any future reprint.

Except as permitted under U.S. Copyright Law, no part of this book may be reprinted, reproduced, transmitted, or utilized in any form by any electronic, mechanical, or other means, now known or hereafter invented, including photocopying, microfilming, and recording, or in any information storage or retrieval system, without written permission from the publishers.

For permission to photocopy or use material electronically from this work, please access www.copyright.com (http://www.copyright.com/) or contact the Copyright Clearance Center, Inc. (CCC), 222 Rosewood Drive, Danvers, MA 01923, 978-750-8400. CCC is a not-for-profit organization that provides licenses and registration for a variety of users. For organizations that have been granted a photocopy license by the CCC, a separate system of payment has been arranged.

Trademark Notice: Product or corporate names may be trademarks or registered trademarks, and are used only for identification and explanation without intent to infringe.

Visit the Taylor & Francis Web site at
http://www.taylorandfrancis.com

and the CRC Press Web site at
http://www.crcpress.com

Contents

Abstract		xi
Prerequisites		xiii
Key Words		xv
Task Statements		xvii

Chapter 1	Understanding the Legal System	1
1.1	Overview of the Court System	1
1.2	State Courts	2
1.3	Federal Courts	3
1.4	An Understanding of the Court System	3
1.5	Lawsuit Procedures	4

Chapter 2	Marketing Consultation Services	5
2.1	Attorney Considerations in Contracting an Expert	5
2.2	Expert Marketing Considerations	6
	2.2.1 Resources Forensic Experts Use for Marketing	7
	2.2.1.1 Social Media	7
	2.2.1.2 Referrals from Other Attorneys	7
	2.2.1.3 Articles, Books, Presentations, and Other Sources on the Topic	7
	2.2.1.4 Client Recommendations	7
	2.2.1.5 Trade Publication Advertisements	7
	2.2.1.6 Professional Legal/Expert Organization Publications	8
	2.2.1.7 Expert Witness Referral Organizations and Professional Directories	8

		2.2.2	Referral Agencies	8
	2.3	Establishing Appropriate Consulting Fees		9
	2.4	Establishing Procedures for Contracts		9
		2.4.1	The Résumé or Curriculum Vitae	10
		2.4.2	Follow Up after the Initial Call	11
			2.4.2.1 Additional Detailed Résumé and Other Information	11
			2.4.2.2 Fee Requirements	11
			2.4.2.3 Retainers	12

Chapter 3 Litigation Processes, Themes, and Strategies — 13

	3.1	Initial Interview of the Attorney and the Potential Client		13
		3.1.1	Attorney Considerations in Deciding to Take a Case	14
		3.1.2	The Initial Attorney Paperwork	15
			3.1.2.1 The Attorney–Client Agreement	15
			3.1.2.2 Authorizations for Client Record Releases	15
	3.2	Attorney Considerations in Deciding to Use a Forensic Expert		16
		3.2.1	Initial Expectations of the Forensic Expert	16
			3.2.1.1 Definition of a Forensic Expert	16
			3.2.1.2 Duties and Qualifications of a Forensic Expert	17
			3.2.1.3 Professionalism, Ethics, Integrity, and Honesty	18
		3.2.2	The Work Product Privilege	19
	3.3	Disclosure Considerations for the Forensic Expert		19
		3.3.1	Conflicts of Interest	19
			3.3.1.1 Identify Whether the Attorney Is Working for the Plaintiff or the Defense	19
			3.3.1.2 Identify Where the Attorney Got Your Name	20
			3.3.1.3 Identify the Issues in the Case	20
			3.3.1.4 Identify Any Insurance Carriers	20
			3.3.1.5 Identify the Parties Involved	20
			3.3.1.6 Identify the Opposing Counsel	21
	3.4	Discovery		21
		3.4.1	Disclosure Statements	22
		3.4.2	Interrogatories	22
		3.4.3	Depositions	23
		3.4.4	Requests for Production of Documents or Physical Inspection	23
		3.4.5	Physical and Mental Examinations	23

		3.4.6	Requests for Admissions	24
		3.4.7	Subpoena	24
		3.4.8	Subpoena Duces Tecum	24
		3.4.9	Motion to Quash	24
		3.4.10	Motion for Protective Order	25
CHAPTER 4	**GENERAL LEGAL PRINCIPLES**			27
	4.1	Federal Rules of Civil Procedure		27
		4.1.1	Rule 26 of the Federal Rules of Civil Procedure	27
			4.1.1.1 Rule 26(a)(1)	28
			4.1.1.2 Rule 26(a)(2)	28
			4.1.1.3 Rule 26(e)	28
		4.1.2	Rule 37 of the Federal Rules of Civil Procedure	28
	4.2	Federal Rules of Evidence		28
		4.2.1	Rule 702 of the Federal Rules of Evidence	29
			4.2.1.1 *Frye* Standard	29
			4.2.1.2 *Daubert* Standard	29
		4.2.2	Rule 703 of the Federal Rules of Evidence	30
		4.2.3	Rule 704 of the Federal Rules of Evidence	30
		4.2.4	Rule 705 of the Federal Rules of Evidence	30
		4.2.5	Rule 706 of the Federal Rules of Evidence	30
	4.3	The Federal Rules of Criminal Procedure		31
		4.3.1	Rule 16 of the Federal Rules of Criminal Procedure	31
	4.4	Motions and the Forensic Expert		31
		4.4.1	The Motion for Summary Judgment	31
		4.4.2	The Motion in Limine	32
		4.4.3	The Motion for Directed Verdict	32
	4.5	Typical Elements of a Negligence Claim		32
		4.5.1	Duty	32
			4.5.1.1 Professional Standard of Care	32
			4.5.1.2 Community or National Standard	33
		4.5.2	Breach of Duty	33
		4.5.3	Proximate Cause	33
		4.5.4	Damages	33
	4.6	Disclosing Notes in Accordance with Federal Rules of Civil Procedure		34
CHAPTER 5	**EXPERT WITNESS PAYMENT**			35
	5.1	The Importance of Retention		35
	5.2	Methods for Collecting Various Consultation Fees		35
		5.2.1	Retainers	35
		5.2.2	Deposition	35
		5.2.3	Trial	36
		5.2.4	Ongoing Billing	36
	5.3	Establishing Appropriate Consultation Fees		36
	5.4	Appropriate Retainer Etiquette		37

CONTENTS

CHAPTER 6	THE DISCOVERY PROCESS		39
6.1	The Attorney's Role		39
6.2	The Forensic Expert's Role		39
	6.2.1	Getting Complete Information	40
	6.2.2	Information Management	40
	6.2.3	Additional Data Collection	41
6.3	The Inspection		41
	6.3.1	Inspection Methods	41
	6.3.2	Inspection Restrictions	42
	6.3.3	Inspection Etiquette	42
6.4	The Formal Written Report or Affidavit		43
	6.4.1	Using Notes	43
	6.4.2	Reviewing All Data	43
	6.4.3	Writing the Report	43
	6.4.4	Goals of the Written Report	44
	6.4.5	Maintaining Credibility	44
6.5	Reading the Subpoena		45
CHAPTER 7	THE FORENSIC EXPERT'S DEPOSITION		47
7.1	Preparing for the Deposition		47
	7.1.1	Timing of the Deposition	47
	7.1.2	Purpose of the Deposition	47
	7.1.3	Communicating with the Attorney	48
		7.1.3.1 Litigation Issues	48
		7.1.3.2 What to Expect at the Deposition	49
	7.1.4	The Role of the Subpoena Duces Tecum	50
	7.1.5	The Practice Session	50
	7.1.6	The Forensic Expert's Files	51
7.2	The Deposition		51
	7.2.1	The Nature of the Testimony	51
		7.2.1.1 Questions regarding Fees	52
		7.2.1.2 Use of Intimidation	52
		7.2.1.3 Use of Objections	53
	7.2.2	Answering Questions	53
		7.2.2.1 Listen Carefully	53
		7.2.2.2 Think before Answering	53
		7.2.2.3 Speak Slowly	54
		7.2.2.4 Correct Mistakes	54
		7.2.2.5 Remain Alert and Focused	54
		7.2.2.6 Stay within Your Area of Expertise	54
		7.2.2.7 Express Opinions Clearly	55
		7.2.2.8 Tell the Truth	55
	7.2.3	The Forensic Expert's Opinions	55
7.3	Conclusion of the Deposition		56
7.4	After the Deposition		57
	7.4.1	Review of the Deposition	57
	7.4.2	Status Check	57

Contents

	7.4.3	Additional Information		57
	7.4.4	Settlement Negotiations		58

Chapter 8 The Trial — 59
- 8.1 The Role of the Forensic Expert in the Trial Strategy — 59
- 8.2 Preparing for Trial — 59
  - 8.2.1 Attorney–Expert Communication — 59
  - 8.2.2 Preparing Technical Information and Exhibits — 60
  - 8.2.3 Preparing for Testimony — 60
  - 8.2.4 Billing before Trial — 61
  - 8.2.5 The Trial Subpoena — 61
- 8.3 The Trial Process — 61
  - 8.3.1 Jury Selection — 62
    - 8.3.1.1 The Judge Questions Potential Jurors — 62
    - 8.3.1.2 The Attorneys Question Potential Jurors—Voir Dire — 62
    - 8.3.1.3 The Attorneys Challenge Potential Jurors — 62
    - 8.3.1.4 The Jury Is Selected — 63
  - 8.3.2 Opening Statements — 63
  - 8.3.3 Giving Testimony — 63
    - 8.3.3.1 Arrive Early — 63
    - 8.3.3.2 Expect to Stay — 64
    - 8.3.3.3 Enter the Courtroom Appropriately — 64
    - 8.3.3.4 Dress Appropriately — 64
    - 8.3.3.5 Know What to Expect — 64
    - 8.3.3.6 Show Respect — 65
  - 8.3.4 Direct Examination of the Forensic Expert — 65
  - 8.3.5 Cross-Examination of the Forensic Expert — 65
  - 8.3.6 The Redirect of the Forensic Expert — 66
  - 8.3.7 The Directed Verdict — 66
  - 8.3.8 The Defense Presents Its Case — 66
  - 8.3.9 Jury Instructions — 67
  - 8.3.10 Closing Arguments — 67
  - 8.3.11 Jury Deliberations — 68
  - 8.3.12 Post-Trial Motions — 68
- 8.4 After the Trial — 68
  - 8.4.1 Obtaining Feedback — 68
    - 8.4.1.1 Jury Feedback — 68
    - 8.4.1.2 Attorney Feedback — 69
    - 8.4.1.3 Client Feedback — 69
  - 8.4.2 Self-Evaluation and Reflections — 69

Chapter 9 Professional Practices — 71
- 9.1 The Role of Credibility, Reputation, and Professional Discipline in Forensic Consulting — 71
  - 9.1.1 Providing a Scientific Foundation — 71

		9.1.2	Methods for Rendering Professional Opinions	71
			9.1.2.1 Be Prepared	72
			9.1.2.2 Be Honest	72
			9.1.2.3 Speak Clearly and Authoritatively	72
			9.1.2.4 Always Stay Calm	72
			9.1.2.5 Do Not Exaggerate	73
			9.1.2.6 Listen Carefully/Answer Thoughtfully	73
			9.1.2.7 Do Not Attack Other Experts	73
			9.1.2.8 Be Professional	73
			9.1.2.9 Keep Conclusions Probable or to a Certainty	73
			9.1.2.10 Be Humble	73
			9.1.2.11 Be Organized	73
	9.2	Stipulating Responsibilities to the Attorney		74
	9.3	Sharing Files Appropriately		74
	9.4	Final Billing		74
	9.5	Concluding on a Good Note		74

ADDITIONAL SOURCES   77

Abstract

In a proper court setting, experts in various fields are asked to provide testimony and evidence on differing professional topics. To be able to effectively testify in a courtroom setting requires knowledge, training, experience, and expertise. The Certified Forensic Consultant (CFC) exam certifies an individual's knowledge of the legal system and court procedures. The exam covers the following topics: the discovery process, the forensic expert's deposition, litigation processes, the trial, general legal principles, professional practices, consultation services, and expert witness payment. Materials presented in this CFC guide will prepare the reader with the necessary information to achieve this goal.

Readers will learn the complete court process, from opening arguments to the conclusion, proper fee establishment, the way to correctly testify in a professional manner, and the forensic expert's role in litigation.

Prerequisites

A candidate must have a minimum of a bachelor's degree with 3 years of experience in a forensic-related field, or 5 years of experience in a forensic-related field.

Key Words

- Jurisprudence
- Jurisdiction
- Negligence
- Prima facie
- Depositions
- Interrogatories
- Requests for production of documents and/or physical inspection
- Requests for admissions
- Motion for summary judgment
- Motion in limine
- Motion to strike
- Subpoena
- Subpoena duces tecum
- Voir dire

Task Statements

- Present suggestions and thoughts concerning specific litigation
- Stipulate responsibilities to attorneys
- Conclude involvement with cases effectively and appropriately
- Define *deposition*
- Describe the timing, potential purposes, and conduct of the deposition
- Explain the role of attorney–client communication in preparing for and giving the deposition
- Explain the importance of practice in preparing for the deposition
- List discovery methods used by attorneys
- Explain the discovery process
- Identify the importance of discovery to attorney theories and strategies
- Explain the forensic expert's role in the discovery process
- Describe the attorney's role in the discovery process
- Explain the role of effective note-taking and filing in the discovery process
- Describe discoverability rules
- Clarify the importance of retaining a copy of all testimonies given
- Explain the importance of consistency in testimony across cases

1
Understanding the Legal System

1.1 Overview of the Court System

The Constitution of the United States mandates separation of powers between the executive, legislative, and judiciary branches of government. The legislative branch enacts laws which are referenced as statutes. The judiciary determines the constitutionality of laws and relies on prior cases to reach decisions which are pending. The executive branch enforces the laws.

When there is a conflict between two or more parties and they cannot come to an agreement, they may utilize the judiciary as a way to resolve the issue. In civil cases, the party who files a complaint is referred to as the plaintiff or petitioner. The party who is served with a complaint has the responsibility of filing an answer and is called the defendant or respondent. These cases involve monetary awards as a means of remuneration or a declaration as to what can be done in a lawful manner. In criminal cases, the public state or municipality brings the action against the defendant and involves a loss of liberty or fines meant to punish criminal wrongdoing.

Once a case is filed, it proceeds to litigation and ultimately may result in a trial. In some cases, a jury may render a decision and, in some cases, the judge would decide the result. Occasionally, one of the parties may file a motion in which the court will rule prior to a trial or during a trial. Motions to dismiss are filed if the court does not have jurisdiction to hear the case or if the complaint does not express a legal theory which can result in a verdict. The judge may rule on a motion for summary judgment if the facts are not in dispute, which would result in a particular finding without the need for a jury or fact finder to render a decision. If the party presenting their case at trial cannot sustain their burden of proof, the judge may direct a verdict in favor of the other party without the necessity of a jury reaching a decision.

1.2 State Courts

Each state in the United States has its own court system. Once a verdict or judgment is rendered in the trial court, either or all of the parties may appeal the case to the state's court of appeals. A common misconception is that a party can file an appeal because of the result; however, there must be legal or evidentiary flaws asserted regarding the judge's rulings before an appeal may be filed. If one or all of the parties believes the Court of Appeals rendered a decision that is incorrect under the existing law, an appeal may be submitted to the state's Supreme Court (except New York, where the New York Supreme Court is the trial court and the Court of Appeals is the final appellate decision maker). The state's Supreme Court can accept or refuse to hear an appeal with the exception of death penalty matters, where the Supreme Court must decide the case on an automatic appeal.

Trial cases are not reported in state court actions. The appellate court can publish or choose not to publish its opinion once there is an appeal. If the appellate court elects to publish its opinion, the holding is precedent for all courts within that same jurisdiction. When a case has precedential value, it should be followed by all the courts and allows litigants and attorneys to be able to forecast the merits of each individual case. If a case is not published, it lacks precedential value but may be used as persuasive.

Sometimes, states have more than one appellate court division. If a state has more than one appellate court division, a decision is precedential within that same division but is only persuasive in other areas within the state. A case that is decided and published by the state's Supreme Court amounts to a precedent for the entire state. A decision by one state may be persuasive in another state but does not set a precedent.

Each state has its own set of evidentiary instructions which are called rules of evidence. Every state's rules of evidence mandate how evidence is presented for trial and what constitutes as an expert. Each state utilizes different criteria for allowing expert opinions at trial.

Each state also has its own set of procedural rules for civil and criminal cases. These rules of civil or criminal procedure dictate discovery rules. Discovery is the process where one party educates the adverse party on its case. Again, each state has different requirements for what must be or does not have to be disclosed to the adverse party.

1.3 Federal Courts

Cases are filed in the federal system when there is sole federal jurisdiction involving a federal statute or enactment. Cases can also be filed with the federal courts when there is a federal question contained within the litigation or if there is diversity of citizenship where the parties reside in different states. The federal courts were initiated under the United States Constitution, Article III.

The federal court system involves district courts, which are the trial courts. The appeal would be directed toward the Circuit Court of Appeals in the area where the district court is located. An appeal from the Circuit Court of Appeals would be filed with the United States Supreme Court, who has the authority to accept or refuse to hear the appeal.

Some district court cases are published but the decisions are not considered to be precedent. These types of citations will be shown in the Federal Supplement by the West Publishing Company. A Circuit Court of Appeals–reported case will be shown in the federal citation with a notation of the circuit from which it is published. A Circuit Court of Appeals–published decision is precedential within that same circuit but is only persuasive in other circuits.

Even though one would think that all federal courts work the same, they do not. Each federal court utilizes local rules and each judge may interpret the federal rules of evidence, criminal, or civil procedure in different ways.

1.4 An Understanding of the Court System

The expert must rely on the attorney to provide information as to the applicable rules of evidence and procedure. Even an expert who practices frequently in a jurisdiction may be surprised when the rules change. The jurisdiction and location will dictate what must be disclosed by the expert and the attorney to the adverse party along with whether communications are privileged, private, or discoverable.

1.5 Lawsuit Procedures

Once the client and attorney elect to litigate the case, a lawsuit is filed. The filing of the lawsuit is instituted by a complaint. Once the adverse party or parties are served, each would file an answer or appropriate motion. One motion that may be filed is a motion to dismiss for such reasons as (1) the claims described in the complaint do not amount to a legal cause of action; (2) the court does not have jurisdiction to render a decision; or (3) the service was not proper. If the adverse party or parties file an answer, the case moves into discovery, which is discussed in detail in Chapter 3.

2

Marketing Consultation Services

2.1 Attorney Considerations in Contracting an Expert

A forensic expert is "a witness who is qualified as an expert by knowledge, skill experience, training, or education" pursuant to Rule 702 of the Federal Rules of Civil Procedure. Attorneys must also consider whether an expert is needed and, if so, how the expert will impact the judge and jury. Academic and/or practical experiences are covered later in this chapter when discussing fees, résumés (curriculum vitae), and federal rules that relate to the forensic expert. Attorneys usually consult with a proposed expert in order to determine opinions and then make an election to utilize the expert as a disclosed testifying expert.

Since attorneys are generally not experts in their particular cases, they may want to hire someone to provide them with information and advice prior to or immediately after meeting with their client or agreeing to accept the case. The attorney may want to understand the case and make a determination as to whether they wish to provide legal counsel or even accept the case and commit time and expenses. If this is the case, the attorney may not be contemplating whether the consulting expert is going to be listed and disclosed as an expert should the case proceed to litigation. Even if the case does proceed to litigation, the attorney may not want to disclose the consulting expert and the expert's identity may be kept private pursuant to Rule 26(b)(4) of the Federal Rules of Civil Procedure. Attorneys utilize different factors in reaching out to expert consultants, such as (1) proposed fees; (2) expertise in the particular area; (3) proposed time frames to accomplish the tasks; and (4) ability to communicate with the attorney in a timely manner.

If the attorney decides that the case has merit and wishes to proceed to litigation, the attorney must determine which experts to disclose to the adverse party or parties. The attorney has to make additional determinations as to whether the expert is optimal to testify, such as (1) training, education, and experience; (2) prior cases in which the expert has been retained and/or testified; (3) expert's fees; (4) appearance of the expert; and (5) the expert's ability to communicate.

2.2 Expert Marketing Considerations

Marketing by experts can include the Internet and direct mail campaigns targeting attorneys, as well as advertisements in legal publications or trade journals. Some experts invite attorneys to demonstrations or seminars where they are presenting or conducting their business. Attorneys must weigh such activities by potential experts in relationship to how they will present the expert at trial. In this chapter, an outline of the business approach to marketing as a forensic expert will be covered. Personalized marketing presents a variety of advantages as well as pitfalls.

The disadvantages of expert marketing:

- The opportunity for opposing counsel to claim that the forensic expert purposely solicits litigation work as opposed to being sought out as a recognized professional in his or her field;
- the forensic expert may appear biased; and
- the forensic expert may derive a large percentage of income from testimony alone, and could be characterized as a *hired gun* rather than a professional in his or her field.

The advantages of expert marketing:

- Professional publications, interviews, professional research, and media exposure at trial are avenues that are recognized as appropriate for marketing expert skills;
- the forensic expert expands his or her participation in legal cases beyond simple word-of-mouth exposure to law firms; and
- the forensic expert can benefit from his or her professional, academic, and practical experience by feeling as if he or she is assisting justice and receiving increased revenue.

2.2.1 Resources Forensic Experts Use for Marketing

Attorneys often consider the following leads when looking for experts.

2.2.1.1 Social Media   Experts should be aware of social media, including websites, networking, and informational sites. Experts need to be aware that every piece of information that is provided through the Internet is a permanent and retrievable communication. Professionalism should be exhibited at all times since messages and pronouncements may be taken out of context.

2.2.1.2 Referrals from Other Attorneys   One of the most effective methods of finding the best forensic expert is to tap into other attorneys' personal experiences in seeing the expert perform. Knowing the expert's integrity, ability to teach, and present opinions to the court, as well as personality and attitude, is critical. A referring attorney can best judge these traits. There are local and national Listservs and databases in which most attorneys participate. The name of a good expert can spread almost instantaneously, while the name of a poor expert can spread just as fast. If the expert has testified in deposition, hearing, or trial, there will most likely be a database in which other attorneys can locate the transcript.

2.2.1.3 Articles, Books, Presentations, and Other Sources on the Topic   Articles are an excellent means to getting an expert's professional expertise out to the trade, profession, and public. Experts can and should write their own articles, books, etc., and lecture at conferences, seminars, workshops, and other forums on a regular basis.

2.2.1.4 Client Recommendations   These are an excellent approach, but the attorney must make sure that such a recommendation will not become troublesome later since the relationship between the client and expert must be purely professional to avoid any conflicts of interest.

2.2.1.5 Trade Publication Advertisements   Trade publication advertisements may suit certain experts over others. It is recommended that good research be done on the publication and the responses to the experts within the publication prior to listing your particular service or profile.

2.2.1.6 Professional Legal/Expert Organization Publications These are excellent journals, since they not only present a short history or synopsis of litigation but also cite the experts involved and possibly their opinions.

2.2.1.7 Expert Witness Referral Organizations and Professional Directories Referral organizations can provide wide exposure for forensic experts to law firms; however, they may charge fees over and beyond the expert's hourly fee. Professional directories for experts range from free company information listings to elaborate profile sites with elaborate fees. Some directories may suit experts differently in the choices of categories and options of profiling their services.

2.2.2 Referral Agencies

Expert referral agencies usually require experts to work exclusively through their agency for billing, retainers, and other financial agreements regarding the referred case. The expert should make sure that there are no conditions in the contract with the attorney that conflict with these caveats. Expert witness referral agencies usually follow a standard process:

- The attorney seeking a specific expert contacts the agency.
- The expert witness agency then calls potential forensic experts to ascertain their specific expertise and willingness to serve as an expert.
- Upon agreement by the forensic expert to serve, the expert witness agency directs the expert to call the attorney and discuss the litigation.
- The forensic expert calls the attorney.

Should the attorney decide to retain the expert, the referral agency will send a contract to the attorney and the expert. This will also include any and all conditions of services, fees, and forms of payment as the litigation process continues. No-fee agencies are especially beneficial for attorneys since there are no additional fees placed upon the expert fees that must be paid by the client's law firm. Therefore, a referral from one of these organizations of a forensic expert is more likely to result in retention based simply on economic concerns.

Another type of expert witness referral may come through professional organizations or associations. These entities will list their members upon approval on a search database that may be accessed by attorneys at no charge. Experts that align themselves through membership of these associations will find that being listed on the search databases will increase their referral network contacts, find excellent continuing education opportunities, and gather all the latest trends in their discipline at scheduled meetings and conferences held by them.

2.3 Establishing Appropriate Consulting Fees

Fees should be set at levels that are reasonable for the field and expertise. Fees should also be consistent for all clients, and once they are set, should not be changed for the pending matter. Some referral agencies charging a finder's fee to locate forensic experts will ask experts to reduce their fees so that the combined costs of the expert and the agency are not as high, making them more attractive to law firms. This practice can create problems for the forensic experts if attorneys learn that fees have been reduced for some firms and not for others.

2.4 Establishing Procedures for Contracts

The forensic expert should read the contract carefully. Be aware that in most of these agreements, there are conditions that may, for example, bar the forensic expert from working with attorneys known to get names of experts from referral agencies and then refuse to pay the agency anything but a finder's fee. Forensic experts should clarify their obligations to both the agency and the attorney to ensure they do not conflict.

For example, the attorney–expert agreement may contain a clause that prohibits the expert from working for an attorney who locates his or her services through an agency. The attorney could then refuse to pay the agency their required fees, shifting the responsibility to the forensic expert. The agency may then take legal action against the expert for breach of contract. It is interesting to note that referral agencies are more likely to file suit against the forensic expert than against the attorney since their contract is with the expert. The agency's position is that the expert has signed a contract with an attorney that conflicts with the agency contract.

Forensic experts, in signing the referral agency contract, appoint the agency as their agent to bill and receive fees from the client law firm. The referral agency retains their fee and remits the balance to the forensic expert. Should the forensic expert be paid directly by the law firm, it is the expert's responsibility as a legal contractor to forward the agency's fee. If the expert does not do so, the agency may file suit for breach of contract.

Since there may be terms that are negotiable with the agency, the forensic expert should not just accept the document as sent. Remember, the forensic expert can always contact an attorney for legal advice.

The attorney will usually give the forensic expert a reasonable amount of time to submit a report or review any discovery documents. If the expert is unable or unwilling to respond within the allotted time frame, he or she should not take on the case. Some forensic experts include in their consulting agreements a stipulation regarding advance notification required for certain tasks such as depositions or trials. The forensic expert should realize, however, that attorneys often request work at the last minute. The forensic expert must be capable and ready to work at that time and provide the needed information.

It is a good idea for the expert to prepare his or her own contract and may be beneficial for the expert to retain an attorney to help draft the legal document. The contract should disclose the scope of work contemplated as well as any time frames and remuneration, including a retainer if required. The contract should be signed by the attorney on behalf of the law firm as well as client. If there is a problem receiving compensation, the expert may have an additional recourse with the attorney's state bar if the attorney signs the contract on behalf of the attorneys or law firm.

2.4.1 The Résumé or Curriculum Vitae

A résumé, often called curriculum vitae or vitae, can work for or against a forensic expert. An excessively long résumé provides the opposing counsel more opportunities to question the expert than may be needed. Too short a résumé and the forensic expert's credibility or expertise may be challenged. While the résumé should include academic degrees, certifications, licenses, employment history, professional memberships, publications, presentations, and any teaching experience that may be relevant, it should also be brief. It is up to the attorney who questions the forensic expert through interrogatories, in deposition, or at trial to request information concerning the specific expertise of the expert beyond what is included in the résumé.

2.4.2 Follow Up after the Initial Call

Good marketing demands that forensic experts follow up after the initial call. Often, however, experts fail to ascertain what other information the attorney may need to make a hiring decision. Follow up should include the following.

2.4.2.1 Additional Detailed Résumé and Other Information Let the attorney know that a more detailed résumé and, if appropriate, a list of the expert's litigation experiences can be sent if requested with a letter outlining any fee schedule and specific requirements.

The expert should be aware that this information may be discoverable and allow the attorney to choose whether or not additional information is necessary. Additionally, written communications may also be discoverable and every formality should be exhibited to show the professional relationship in the best light possible.

2.4.2.2 Fee Requirements The letter of retention or engagement from the attorney makes the forensic expert a formal part of the litigation and offers some legal protection to ensure payment of all fees and expenses as stated. Never assume that an expert's fees, expenses, or other costs are understood unless they are in writing. Each fee should be delineated in the contract if there are different fees requested, such as (1) review of materials; (2) communications with counsel; (3) travel; (4) deposition testimony; and (5) trial testimony. Many experts, but not all, charge additional fees for deposition or trial testimony. Some experts charge a block of time for testimony since they may have to calendar for an unknown amount of time. Some states, such as California, mandate the expert be paid prior to the deposition for the proposed deposition testimony. If the adverse attorney is paying for the expert's time, that commitment should be commemorated in writing or on the transcript in case there is a dispute over the payment.

The expert should be aware that the adverse attorney will point out that the expert is a paid expert and the forensic expert should not be defensive about charging for services rendered. Jurors generally do not expect experts to render opinions for free but the expert should be aware that exorbitant bills are troublesome.

2.4.2.3 Retainers In addition to a base fee, it may be appropriate for the forensic expert to charge an up-front retainer fee, in full or in part, against the initial hourly charge. Some forensic experts require this retainer fee, or portion thereof, to see if the attorney is serious about using the expert for consulting. The fee also serves as payment to the forensic expert for use of the expert's name in the disclosure documents that will be given to opposing counsel. The retainer may be refundable if not utilized to the full extent or nonrefundable since the expert is taking time and removing the ability to be hired on other cases during that time. In either case, the retainer should be fully explained in the retention agreement since attorneys and experts do not like to be surprised by unanticipated fees.

3
Litigation Processes, Themes, and Strategies

3.1 Initial Interview of the Attorney and the Potential Client

The trial court may appoint an attorney if the case is a criminal matter or a client may wish to retain a private attorney in a civil or criminal matter. If the client choses to meet with the counsel, the attorney may want to conduct an investigation before agreeing to be retained or choosing to sign a retention agreement. Experienced trial attorneys attempt to involve experts in the case prior to the filing of a lawsuit if possible. As discussed earlier, the expert may be retained as a consultant who is to assist the attorney or may be hired to actually be involved in litigation.

Prior to commencement of litigation (claimant) or after a lawsuit has been filed (defense), the attorney hopefully discusses the matter with the client. The client usually, but not always, tells the attorney truthful information about the incident, damage, or loss.

Hopefully, a contemplative attorney listens and then asks the client a series of questions with the expectation that the client will be honest. The attorney should explain the confidential and fiduciary nature of the relationship with the client so that the client will feel comfortable providing truthful information. These questions are designed to obtain information the attorney needs to determine if the potential client has a course of action and whether that course of action is worthwhile (claimant) or determines viable defenses. Often, the attorney will play devil's advocate or will understand and explain the alternative point of view.

There are a number of reasons why the legal system can work only if there is confidentiality with the client. If the attorney does not receive adequate and honest information, the client's case is in jeopardy. If the attorney is taking a civil case on a contingency agreement, the attorney is utilizing time and money without any promise of payment at the end of the matter should the case be lost. If the case is a civil or criminal defense case, the attorney needs honest and complete answers to mount a viable defense.

The attorney should be using the five *w*'s, i.e., *who*, *what*, *where*, *when*, and *why*. The better and more experienced attorneys listen to the answers and, more importantly, evaluate the responses to determine if there is more information that needs to be gleaned. Contrary to some common beliefs, attorneys are people. Attorneys should utilize common sense to determine if the information is believable just as jurors make that determination should the case proceed to trial.

3.1.1 Attorney Considerations in Deciding to Take a Case

Attorneys must determine whether the financial costs and time spent involved in a case are acceptable. The attorney must consider if the potential client will win enough to pay all costs and still receive reasonable compensation for his or her losses or if the client has a viable defense in light of the evidence.

Attorneys must also weigh their law firm's cost of doing business and explain to the client the estimated fees. There are infrequent times when an attorney may accept a case based upon principle or philosophy. The attorney owes the same fiduciary responsibilities to the client if the result is not cost effective. The social impact of such a case, however, may be reason enough to pursue it. In cases where circumstances illustrate that state laws are inappropriate or unreasonable and may need modification, change, or elimination, attorneys may have moral, ethical, or social justification for taking the case.

For instance, an attorney may want to take on a significant injury or medical malpractice case despite a mandatory cap in order to bring attention to an equitable injustice. In Colorado, for example, a tour bus accident killed or permanently injured several people. State road construction crews working on a mountainside accidentally dislodged a boulder, sending it crashing down into the bus. The state was clearly at fault, but Colorado statutes prohibited the injured parties and the families of the deceased to pursue litigation beyond the statutory limit.

LITIGATION PROCESSES, THEMES, AND STRATEGIES

The state's total exposure was $400,000 for all claims; the maximum that each claimant could recover was just $150,000.

This minimal damage award outraged the public. Members of the Colorado Trial Lawyers Association donated their time pro bono to challenge the statutory limits. The governor and legislature agreed that the law was unacceptable. Although their challenge failed in the courts, the result was that the public outcry caused the legislature to amend the statute. Through the efforts of the legal system, laws can be changed to be more reasonable for the public.

3.1.2 The Initial Attorney Paperwork

Attorneys must execute various legal documents when beginning a case, the first of which is the retention agreement, a contract that memorializes the attorney–client relationship.

3.1.2.1 The Attorney–Client Agreement
This agreement typically includes

- Names of the parties
- The scope of the representation
- The attorney's compensation and any retainer
- When costs should be paid and by whom
- Alternatives should the relationship be terminated by either the client or attorney

3.1.2.2 Authorizations for Client Record Releases
The attorney then proceeds with various other documents, including authorizations for client record releases. These can include

- Medical records
- Employment records
- Insurance records
- School records
- Military records
- Criminal history records
- Social Security records
- Worker's compensation records

3.2 Attorney Considerations in Deciding to Use a Forensic Expert

The attorney must now decide if the case requires a consulting expert. The consulting expert is a person with special skills or knowledge in a particular subject who can help the attorney understand the intricacies of the case related to that subject. Such a specialist, often known as a *forensic expert*, must have a fundamental grasp of the attorney–client process.

3.2.1 Initial Expectations of the Forensic Expert

The forensic expert provides the scientific foundation critical to the case and must understand both the client's arguments and the general legal principles involved in the case. The forensic expert is not an advocate for the client and should conduct work as an independent and objective participant whose job is to educate the jury or trier of fact. The forensic expert should explain what evidence would be helpful to communicate opinions should the case go to trial so that the attorney can disclose that evidence or let the adverse party know that the expert intends to utilize demonstrative evidence, which is evidence that assists in explanation but is not intended to be introduced to the jury.

3.2.1.1 Definition of a Forensic Expert The American College of Forensic Examiners Institute defines a *forensic expert* as "a professional who performs an orderly analysis, investigation, inquiry, test, inspection, or examination in an attempt to obtain the truth and form an expert opinion. Almost every scientific and technical field has a forensic application. A forensic examination refers to that part of a professional's practice that is carried out to provide an expert opinion."

Whether or not a person can be deemed a forensic expert is dependent upon the specific subject, court, or case. Rule 702 of the Federal Rules of Evidence provides guidance to the judge as to who is qualified as an expert to be presented at trial. A person deemed a forensic expert in a particular area may be deemed an expert in one court or case but not another. Once an expert is excluded from testifying in one court, the preclusion may be the basis for a motion to strike in another court.

LITIGATION PROCESSES, THEMES, AND STRATEGIES

The American College of Forensic Examiners Institute mandates the following creed for forensic experts:

- I shall investigate for the truth.
- I shall report only the truth.
- I shall avoid conflicts of advocacies.
- I shall conduct myself ethically.
- I shall seek to preserve the highest standard of my profession.
- As a Forensic Examiner, I shall not have a monetary interest in any outcome of a matter in which I am retained.
- I shall share my knowledge and experience with other examiners in a professional manner.
- I shall avoid conflicts of interest and will continue my professional development throughout my career through continuing education, seminars, and other studies.
- As a Forensic Examiner, I will express my expert opinion based only upon my knowledge, skill, education, training, and experience.
- The light of knowledge shall guide me to the truth, and with justice, the truth shall prevail.

3.2.1.2 Duties and Qualifications of a Forensic Expert   A forensic expert must be revealed during the discovery process. Many civil cases do not advance to trial, and are settled after the discovery process.

Due to the Federal Rules of Civil Procedure, a timely report must be designed by the proposed expert during the discovery process. The report must include the information the expert reviewed, their opinions, and the reasons behind their opinions. Additionally, the expert may be required to provide proof of his or her qualifications, a list of previous trials in which he or she has testified, fees and compensation, and any exhibits that may be used in the trial. The expert may be cross-examined during trial when opposing counsel addresses the questions in the deposition. Sometimes experts are served with a subpoena duces tecum, which requires them to bring specific papers and other items identified in the subpoena.

Experts should not be advocates. They should provide honest, unbiased answers. If the forensic expert is asked by an attorney to support an opinion that is not the expert's opinion, the expert should professionally refuse.

The judge chooses which experts are and are not allowed to testify. The judge determines if the expert testimony can provide enough support and value to the case. A judge often allows an expert based upon skills, training, knowledge, and experience. College education is often considered but not always required. Most importantly, the judge allows experts who base opinions on reliable data and who use relevant principles and methodologies to prove the validity of their information.

The opinion of an expert may be based on firsthand knowledge, but this is not usually necessary. Sometimes the expert will discern an opinion based upon records and publications, or even based on evidence or witnesses that are presented at trial. The expert may be asked by the court to state facts, opinions, and assumptions, but may also be asked to formulate expert opinions based on hypothetical information offered by the counsel. Experts should be careful when creating their opinions without an accurate conviction as to the accuracy.

Once an expert is chosen, he or she must treat the case as confidential and decline any comments on the case during the litigation process.

An expert must be prepared to be cross-examined by the opposing counsel, and must be honest in all opinions and responses.

3.2.1.3 Professionalism, Ethics, Integrity, and Honesty The expert must conform to high levels of integrity and professionalism through the deposition and throughout the trial. The expert must carefully listen to and answer questions whether he or she is undergoing direct or cross-examination. The expert must ask for clarification for a question, and not attempt to interject an answer to a question that may be unclear or that he or she does not understand. He or she must also correct any errors that may or may not have been stated in the question.

Immunity for experts in court cases has eroded considerably in recent years. Now, an expert can be held liable for willful misconduct or negligence when forming opinions. Some jurisdictions still allow immunity, but it is becoming more qualified and less absolute. Qualified immunity will not protect experts in situations of misconduct and negligence.

3.2.2 The Work Product Privilege

The work product privilege is a statute or rule that protects the attorney's own personal notes, investigations, and contacts with consulting experts from having to be disclosed to the opposing counsel. Disclosure of such items at this point in the litigation process would compromise and interfere with the attorney's thought process. This privilege is waived, however, if the attorney provides the expert with privileged information.

3.3 Disclosure Considerations for the Forensic Expert

Although the attorney may be brief in explaining the basic issues of the litigation, forensic experts must be willing to elaborate on their expertise, experience, and willingness to serve as an expert. The initial call after an attorney has located a possible candidate may well be the most critical point in the communication between attorney and forensic expert.

3.3.1 Conflicts of Interest

During the initial interview, the expert *must* tell the attorney about any potential conflicts of interest or problems the forensic expert may face if retained. Conflicts of interest can include philosophical differences of opinion, previous testimony, or a previous relationship with the opposing parties.

3.3.1.1 Identify Whether the Attorney Is Working for the Plaintiff or the Defense This information is a basic starting point for the forensic expert. Some experts work exclusively for one side or the other and they need to know whom the attorney is representing before discussing any confidential information. The forensic expert has an ethical responsibility at this time to decide whether he or she can assist the litigation, based on the information presented in the case.

The American Board of Forensic Examiners assists in this area. Its mission is to "advance the profession of forensic examination and consultation across the many professional fields of our membership by elevating standards through education, basic and advanced training, and Board Certifications." The college serves as a national center for this purpose and disseminates information and knowledge by lectures, seminars, conferences, workshops, Internet, World Wide Web, distance courses, and publications.

Forensic experts can find out more about law firms seeking their expertise by consulting the Martindale-Hubbell Law Directory, which is available online.

3.3.1.2 Identify Where the Attorney Got Your Name The opposing counsel will probably ask how the hiring attorney first contacted the forensic expert. The answer to this question is important. In addition to affecting the credibility of the forensic expert, it helps the expert evaluate his or her marketing efforts and determine whether or not to accept the case, especially if the referral came from another attorney.

3.3.1.3 Identify the Issues in the Case A brief explanation of the claims and legal position of the attorney is helpful at this point. Discuss the legal grounds of the lawsuit. The more forensic experts know about the arguments from both sides, the better they understand the critical issues about which they are being asked to render an opinion. Forensic experts need to know where their retaining attorney is in the discovery process, and should ask increasingly more detailed questions as they proceed with their evaluation of the presented facts. The credibility and impact of the forensic expert's testimony can be jeopardized if an opinion is rendered before he or she has adequate information.

3.3.1.4 Identify Any Insurance Carriers Forensic experts need to know what insurance carriers are involved in the case to prevent conflicts of interest. The insurance carrier may already be paying the expert to serve on a different case. Also, if the expert is working for the plaintiff, for example, the insurance company representing the defendant may well decide to eliminate the expert as a possible witness in future litigation. Forensic experts often choose not to work for certain insurance companies for a variety of reasons, or may have had some past situation involving the insurance company that the attorney needs to know at this time.

3.3.1.5 Identify the Parties Involved The forensic expert must know who the parties are to avoid any potential conflicts of interest. The forensic expert may have a certain bias or have had a previous experience

LITIGATION PROCESSES, THEMES, AND STRATEGIES

or relationship with one or more of the parties that could damage his or her credibility or affect the impact of opinions or testimony at trial. Some forensic experts prefer not to testify against certain agencies, professional or trade organizations, schools, or public entities. These restrictions should be discussed with the attorney before any confidential information is divulged.

3.3.1.6 Identify the Opposing Counsel The forensic expert must also know who the opposing counsel is to avoid potential conflicts of interest. The expert may have worked for the attorney in previous litigation, which may not always conflict, but it is the responsibility of the forensic expert to reveal this information. The forensic expert may also feel biased or prejudiced due to previous experiences with the opposing counsel.

3.4 Discovery

Discovery is the process mandated by law that allows one side to find out much of what the other side knows and will present at trial. The purpose of discovery is meant to prevent courtroom surprises often depicted in popular media. Discovery is accomplished via a variety of methods and documents. Discovery varies widely between different states and the federal courts.

The formal procedures used by parties to a lawsuit to obtain information before a trial is called discovery. Discovery helps a party find out the other side's version of the facts, what witnesses know, what an expert's opinion is, what documents will be utilized at trial, and other evidence. Rules dictating the allowable methods of discovery have been set up by Congress (for federal courts) and by state legislatures (for state courts).

The scope of information obtainable through discovery is quite broad and not limited to what can be used in a trial. Federal courts and most state courts allow a party to discover any information "reasonably calculated to lead to the discovery of admissible evidence." Because of this broad standard, parties may disagree about what information must be exchanged and what may be kept confidential. These disputes are resolved through the parties agreeing to confidentiality agreements and orders or court rulings on discovery motions.

Part of the pretrial litigation process during which each party requests relevant information and documents from the other side in an attempt to discover pertinent facts. Generally, discovery devices include depositions, interrogatories, requests for admissions, requests for production, and requests for inspection.

3.4.1 Disclosure Statements

Rule 26 of the Federal Rules of Civil Procedure dictates the federal mandate for disclosures. Generally, the Federal Rules are not as stringent as state rules regarding what must be disclosed to the adverse party; however, every state has varying rules. The purpose of the disclosure statements is to allow the adverse party to understand the case to assist in preparation of discovery and ultimately for trial. The federal rules mandate the disclosure to the adverse party the following information: (1) names, addresses, and information of potential persons with knowledge; (2) document utilized to bolster its position; (3) damages claimed; (4) any insurance agreements; and (5) expert reports. The federal rules, unlike many state rules, exempts the following: (1) administrative review actions; (2) an action brought without an attorney; (3) an action to enforce or quash a subpoena; (4) an action for benefit payments; (5) an action to collect a guaranteed student loan; and (6) an ancillary proceeding in a different court.

3.4.2 Interrogatories

Rule 33 of the Federal Rules of Civil Procedure discusses the use of interrogatories. Interrogatories contain questions presented by one side and answered, under verification, by the opposing side. The interrogatories are usually, but not always, served and responded to before any depositions are taken. Interrogatories are only presented to the parties but may involve questions about the adverse party's experts, including prior cases. Again, even if the requested questions may not be admissible in court, the standard is whether the answers could "reasonably lead to the admission of evidence."

3.4.3 Depositions

Rules 27, 28, and 30 of the Federal Rules of Civil Procedure discuss the utilization of depositions. Depositions are sworn statements in which the deponent is administered an oath by the court reporter. The testimony is taken down verbatim by the court reporter. The difference is that there is not a judge present to rule on objections during the deposition itself.

Depositions are sworn statements taken under oath with a court reporter present. Depositions may be taken by videotape if notice is provided. A deposition transcript does not depict the length of time for the response; however, a videotaped deposition shows the response time and shows the mannerisms of the deponent. While some states allow for deposition transcripts to be read or video depositions to be shown during trial, the federal rules allow for the jury to obtain the testimony if (1) the party was present or represented; (2) it complies with the Federal Rules of Evidence; and (3) it is utilized to impeach against a party opponent or the witness is rendered unavailable.

3.4.4 Requests for Production of Documents or Physical Inspection

Rule 34 of the Federal Rules of Civil Procedure allows for the procedure should a party wish to receive specific documents or conduct a physical inspection. Experts are often utilized to inform the attorney as to what documents to request or what to inspect. If a physical inspection is required, the retaining attorney may request the presence of the expert.

3.4.5 Physical and Mental Examinations

Rule 35 of the Federal Rules of Civil Procedure mandates the federal procedure for procuring a mental or physical examination that has been commonly referred to as an independent medical or psychological examination. A federal Rule 35 examination may be made by stipulation of the parties or by motion for good cause in which the mental or physical condition of the party is in issue.

3.4.6 Requests for Admissions

Rule 36 of the Federal Rules of Civil Procedure allows for the use of requests for admission. The purpose of requests for admissions is to limit the issues so that the jury or trier of fact only has to hear the issues in dispute. There are very stringent time frames to respond to requests for admissions and the requests may automatically be deemed admitted if a response is not rendered on time.

3.4.7 Subpoena

Rule 45 of the Federal Rules of Civil Procedure establishes the guidelines for issuing subpoenas. A subpoena is an order telling a witness to appear in at a specified time and place, which includes an office, deposition, or court. A subpoena is issued by the court, although it may be signed by an attorney involved in the matter that compels the witness to comply or to be held in contempt of court.

3.4.8 Subpoena Duces Tecum

This is an order compelling a witness or custodian of records to submit certain documents to a party or to bring them to a scheduled deposition. A subpoena duces tecum is issued by the court, and if the witness fails to comply, the person can be held in contempt. Often, a subpoena duces tecum is served to a custodian of records with a confirmatory letter that the person does not have to attend as long as the documents are produced in full. The expert needs to review the documents to determine if attendance is required and should consult with the retaining attorney.

3.4.9 Motion to Quash

If the expert or retaining attorney objects to certain documents being provided by the expert, the expert can file an objection or the attorney may file a motion to quash. There must be good communication with the retaining attorney as to the process and goals. For instance, there may be a subpoena requesting financial documentation of the expert and the expert may find that request obtrusive. Instead of failing to comply with the subpoena, the expert may want to file an objection and allow the court to decide whether the information may be compelled. In this case, the expert may need to hire independent counsel. However, the retaining attorney may want to file a motion to quash so that the expert does not have to hire independent counsel.

3.4.10 Motion for Protective Order

Rule 26(c)(1)(D) of the Federal Rules of Civil Procedure permits a party to request a protective order in an attempt to forbid inquiry into certain discovery matters such as a request for financial documentation of an expert where the purpose of the request is to harass.

4
GENERAL LEGAL PRINCIPLES

4.1 Federal Rules of Civil Procedure

The most recent Federal Rules of Civil Procedure were effective as of September 1, 2013, and are continually amended concerning discovery and expert disclosures. The Federal Rules of Civil Procedure dictate the procedures by which attorneys handle a case from the filing of a lawsuit, service of a lawsuit, discovery, motions and pleadings, and trial. Some states follow some of the Federal Rules of Civil Procedure in whole and in part, and it is incumbent on the expert to discuss the applicable rules with the retaining expert in the jurisdiction where the case is pending.

4.1.1 Rule 26 of the Federal Rules of Civil Procedure

Rule 26, entitled *General Provisions Governing Discovery*, provides that the duty of disclosure affects the discovery of experts by mandated disclosure without a formal discovery request. It also requires everyone, either hired as an expert witness or employed to regularly provide expert testimony, to produce a report. Except as otherwise directed by the court, each party must serve a complete written report signed by the expert containing

- A complete statement of all opinions and the basis and reasons
- The data or other information considered by the witness in forming the opinion
- Any exhibits to be used to summarize or support the opinions
- The qualifications of the witness, including all publications authored by the witness within the past 10 years
- The compensation to be paid
- A list of all cases in which the witnesses testified during the preceding 4 years

4.1.1.1 Rule 26(a)(1) The parties submit initial disclosure statements and have a continual duty to supplement their disclosures. The disclosures are to provide the case or defense to the adverse party to prevent any surprises at trial.

4.1.1.2 Rule 26(a)(2) The parties must disclose experts and their proposed testimony. A report must be submitted unless stipulated otherwise by the parties. The report must include (1) a complete statement of all opinions and the basis and reasons for them; (2) the facts or data considered; (3) any exhibits used to support the opinions; (4) qualifications including publications authored over the last 10 years; (5) list of other cases in which the expert has provided testimony during the previous 4 years; and (6) compensation.

4.1.1.3 Rule 26(e) The party has a continuing duty to supplement disclosures, including expert reports up to 30 days prior to trial.

4.1.2 Rule 37 of the Federal Rules of Civil Procedure

Rule 26(b)(4)(A) of the Federal Rules of Civil Procedure provides parties the right to depose an expert expected to be called at trial. The deposition can be taken after the report is disclosed. Each jurisdiction has differing requirements as to the time frame for taking an expert's deposition; however, it is ultimately up to the judge to make the decision if the parties cannot reach an agreement.

4.2 Federal Rules of Evidence

The Federal Rules of Evidence are continually amended and concern general rules that the trial court should follow for the admissibility of evidence. The Federal Rules of Evidence are utilized by the federal courts to determine what evidence is admissible. Some states follow some of the Federal Rules of Evidence in whole or in part, and it is incumbent on the expert to discuss the applicable rules with the retaining expert in the jurisdiction where the case is pending.

4.2.1 Rule 702 of the Federal Rules of Evidence

Rule 702 is the qualifying guideline for expert testimony. "A witness who is qualified as an expert by knowledge, skill, experience, training, or education may testify" if it "will help the trier of fact to understand the evidence."

4.2.1.1 Frye *Standard* As science advanced during the 20th century, the legal system "attempted to develop coherent tests for the admissibility of scientific evidence." The first notable development occurred in 1923 with the issuance of the landmark decision in *Frye versus United States*, 293 F. 1013 (D.C. Cir. 1923), a federal case decided by the District of Columbia Circuit in 1923. In *Frye*, the District of Columbia Circuit considered the admissibility of testimony based on the systolic blood pressure test, a precursor of the modern polygraph. The court announced that a novel scientific technique "must be sufficiently established to have gained general acceptance in the particular field in which it belongs" (D.C. Cir. 1923 at 1014). The court found that the systolic test had "not yet gained such standing and scientific recognition among physiological and psychological authorities" (D.C. Cir. 1923). Under the *Frye* standard, it is not enough that a qualified expert or experts testify that a particular technique is valid. Scientific evidence is allowed into the courtroom if it is generally accepted by the relevant scientific community. *Frye* imposes a special burden: the technique must be *generally* accepted by the relevant scientific community.

4.2.1.2 Daubert *Standard* The federal courts and many state courts now follow the standard which was enunciated by the United States Supreme Court in *Daubert versus Merrell Dow Pharms.*, 509 U.S. 579, 113 S. Ct. 2786 (1993). The United States Supreme Court indicated that the judge who must utilize Rule 702 must determine that the expert relied on "scientifically valid principles" before the testimony should be admitted to a jury. The U.S. Supreme Court stated:

> Faced with a proffer of expert scientific testimony under Rule 702, the trial judge, pursuant to Rule 104(a) must make a preliminary assessment of

whether the testimony's underlying reasoning or methodology is scientifically valid and properly can be applied to the facts at issue. Many considerations will bear on the inquiry, including whether the theory or technique in question can be (and has been) tested, whether it has been subjected to peer review and publication, its known or potential error rate and the existence and maintenance of standards controlling its operation, and whether it has attracted widespread acceptance within a relevant scientific community. The inquiry is a flexible one, and its focus must be solely on principles and methodology, not on the conclusions that they generate.

4.2.2 Rule 703 of the Federal Rules of Evidence

Rule 703 is the guideline as to what constitutes the basis of an expert's opinion. "An expert may base an opinion on facts or data in the case that the expert has been made aware of or personally observed. If experts in the particular field would reasonably rely on those kinds of facts or data in forming an opinion on the subject, they need not be admissible for the opinion to be admitted." The probative value of the opinion must outweigh any prejudicial effect.

4.2.3 Rule 704 of the Federal Rules of Evidence

An expert can testify as to an ultimate issue of fact. However, there is an exception in criminal cases where the expert cannot testify as to whether the criminal defendant had the requisite mental state if that is an element of the crime.

4.2.4 Rule 705 of the Federal Rules of Evidence

Rule 705 of the Federal Rules of Evidence has been amended to conform with Rule 26(a)(2)(B) of the Federal Rules of Civil Procedure. Any data provided to an expert or found by the expert are not privileged and are discoverable.

4.2.5 Rule 706 of the Federal Rules of Evidence

Rule 706 details court-appointed expert witnesses who deal primarily with criminal matters. The court can appoint an expert by agreement of the parties or each side may hire its own experts. It allows for the deposition of the expert witness.

4.3 The Federal Rules of Criminal Procedure

4.3.1 Rule 16 of the Federal Rules of Criminal Procedure

Rule 16 of the Federal Rules of Criminal Procedure discusses the disclosure of relevant evidence, witnesses, and expert witnesses. Each state has its own disclosure requirements which do not necessarily follow the Federal Rules of Criminal Procedure. The expert should discuss the applicable rules with the retaining attorney.

4.4 Motions and the Forensic Expert

It is vital for the forensic expert to be aware of and understand the following motions since they can affect the expert's testimony: motions for summary and motions in limine. The communication between the forensic expert and the hiring attorney must be clear on these matters. Attorneys are officers of the court and have a duty to explain to their forensic experts exactly what the court rulings are and how they may affect the expert's testimony. For instance, a forensic expert who does not know about or understand a rule on a motion could make an inappropriate comment during testimony and be admonished by the judge or cause a mistrial. One sensitive area involves mentioning *insurance* in litigations that involve insurance companies that may be forced to pay damages. A forensic expert's reference to insurance can be enough, in certain situations, to cause a mistrial.

4.4.1 The Motion for Summary Judgment

The motion for summary judgment is an argument made by one party that there is no dispute of fact or law, and therefore, the judge should rule as a matter of law that one or all claims be disposed of by the court.

Summary judgment proceedings are governed by Rule 56, Federal Rules of Civil Procedure. "A party against whom a claim, counterclaim, or cross-claim is asserted or a declaratory judgment is sought may, at any time, move . . . for a summary judgment in the party's favor as to all or any part thereof. The judgment sought shall be rendered forthwith if the pleadings, depositions, answers to interrogatories, and admissions on file, together with the affidavits, if any, show that there is no genuine issue as to any material fact and that the moving party is entitled to a judgment as a matter of law."

4.4.2 *The Motion in Limine*

The motion in limine is fundamentally a motion to prevent an opposing party from introducing into evidence or mentioning in front of a jury a particular fact. Generally, motions in limine are decided before trial so that an attorney does not make an inappropriate comment during opening statements or is precluded from attempting to introduce evidence in front of a jury.

4.4.3 *The Motion for Directed Verdict*

The directed verdict is an attempt by the defense to argue that the adverse party failed to prove a prima facie case or defense and did not present any issues of fact that would require jury consideration.

4.5 Typical Elements of a Negligence Claim

Forensic experts, in rendering their opinions and conclusions, may be asked to address some or all of the following elements during their testimony. For this reason alone, the forensic expert should be aware of claims in other litigations that illustrate how these four elements were presented.

4.5.1 *Duty*

Duty pertains to whether the defendant has a legal responsibility to the plaintiff. For instance, a motorist has a legal duty owed to other drivers, passengers, and pedestrians.

4.5.1.1 Professional Standard of Care The professional standard of care is the level of care that is promulgated by the profession itself and may be community based or nationally/internationally based as in the case of a board-certified professional. This can be illustrated by position papers, research and standards, or practice as recommended, suggested, or required by professional and/or trade organizations within a profession or industry. Much of the forensic expert's testimony will be based on these standards, or any standards that were not met, as they relate to the evidence reviewed.

4.5.1.2 Community or National Standard If the party is a nationally board-certified professional, the standard of care is national. If the party is state board certified, it is usually a statewide standard of care. If the party is not certified, it is generally a community standard of care. For example, a non–board-certified physician in a rural area who is a general practitioner is typically held to the standard of care of a like physician in a rural area, while a board-certified surgeon would be held to a national standard of care.

4.5.2 Breach of Duty

Breach of duty reflects the evidence that such a duty was not carried out. This breach of duty can vary from a car accident where a person's driving skills as a citizen are in question, to a higher level of duty, or breach of duty, regarding a professional standard of care.

4.5.3 Proximate Cause

The proximate cause issue is where the plaintiff establishes that the actual damages occurred as a result of the claimed breach of duty. Damages are the injury or loss claimed to have been suffered by the plaintiff. In a case involving physical injury, this is usually where a medical health provider will testify.

While the forensic expert's testimony will deal with the issues of duty, breach of duty, and proximate cause, the expert will testify as to the proximate cause of the injury to "a reasonable degree of medical/scientific probability."

4.5.4 Damages

The party making a claim has the burden to prove that the duty breached caused an actual injury or pecuniary damage. Additionally, there is generally a higher burden of proof to submit a claim for punitive damages, which are damages that are meant to punish the wrongdoer and prevent others from the same conduct.

4.6 Disclosing Notes in Accordance with Federal Rules of Civil Procedure

The forensic expert should discuss with the retaining attorney whether to keep notes. Notes may save time and help provide the basis for rendering opinions and preparing reports; however, many attorneys do not want their experts cross-examined on their notes and many experts do not want to keep notes.

These notes are part of the forensic expert's formal files and, as such, are discoverable. This means the forensic expert must disclose these notes, in addition to all other items that appear in the expert's files, to opposing counsel if requested.

Files may be needed or requested by attorneys in future litigation. They may also be required as production of documents under the new Federal Rules of Civil Procedure discussed earlier.

5

Expert Witness Payment

5.1 The Importance of Retention

The expert should send a written commemoration of fee requirements and any other specific billing or operations requirements the attorney may need before agreeing to retain the expert. The letter of retention is discoverable and offers some legal protection to ensure payment of all fees and expenses as stated. Attorneys must know that the expert expects prompt payment of fees, expenses, and other costs in an agreed-upon fashion. At times, attorneys will wait for an insurance payment or receivables (sometimes this can take months) before forwarding the forensic expert's payment. This arrangement is fine provided that both the attorney and the expert agree.

5.2 Methods for Collecting Various Consultation Fees

5.2.1 Retainers

It is appropriate for the forensic expert to charge an up-front retainer fee against the initial hourly charge prior to commencing any work. Some forensic experts require this retainer fee before commencing any work.

5.2.2 Deposition

The forensic expert is a professional who should be paid for services rendered at the time or before such services. It is always best to receive written assurances as to the amount of payment prior to agreeing to a deposition. If there is no written commemoration of payment, a discussion regarding how to resolve the matter should be conducted while the court reporter is inscribing the conversation.

The forensic expert should also discuss the predeposition fees with the retaining attorney. The forensic expert needs to be prepared for the testimony and needs to keep the attorney informed as to the costs to prepare.

Additionally, different jurisdictions have different rules and procedures as to the costs of travel to and from depositions. Again, this should be discussed with the retaining attorney prior to the deposition.

5.2.3 Trial

Prior to trial, the forensic experts should provide their retaining attorney with a complete billing for all professional consulting services rendered at that time. The billing is discoverable and should be descriptive enough for the retaining attorney to understand the tasks completed.

5.2.4 Ongoing Billing

The forensic expert should normally bill on a regular basis, which should be discussed with the retaining attorney. Regular billing is critical to the litigation process since the parties in the litigation may be engaged in settlement discussions and the forensic expert's costs will probably be calculated into any financial agreement.

5.3 Establishing Appropriate Consultation Fees

Identify any state laws regulating how a forensic expert can be paid. Some states frown upon a forensic expert charging a flat fee and a flat fee may be problematic for the expert as grounds for cross-examination. This information should be discussed so billings can be made appropriately for services rendered.

Fees should be set at levels that are reasonable for the expert's field and level of expertise. Fees can be based on the following criteria:

- Formal education (i.e., bachelor's, master's, or doctoral degrees)
- Formal professional positions held
- Practical experiences in the field of study or discipline

- Practical experiences as a forensic expert or expert witness
- Professional authorship including books, articles, texts, and interviews
- Public/professional name recognition as a recognized expert
- Time away from regular professional employment while testifying and performing duties associated with the case

Of course, the fees are subject to agreement of the parties, or ultimately by the judge, if one of the parties moves to have the fees adjusted.

5.4 Appropriate Retainer Etiquette

A forensic expert should do only those professional tasks requested by the attorney. If additional work such as research is required, the expert should receive written approval from the attorney first, with an agreed upon time limit.

Once the retainer is exhausted, the expert can request a subsequent retainer if this has been agreed to with the retaining attorney. The expert should always request both oral and written confirmation if the attorney has requested consulting work that will require significant time and expense.

6
THE DISCOVERY PROCESS

6.1 The Attorney's Role

The courts' liberal discovery policies encourage both sides to become knowledgeable about the issues, facts, and value of their positions. The best resolution is the parties agreeing to a settlement without the ultimate need for trial, which is a risk for all parties. The litigation system is designed for trials only in cases in which reasonable parties cannot reach an agreement so as to alleviate the vast number of cases, time, and expense.

During the discovery process, attorneys for each side gather information pertinent to the case. This is a fact-finding effort, and the information helps attorneys determine theories and strategies as they proceed with the litigation. The discovery process takes on many forms. Both the attorney and the forensic expert must approach this process in a systematic manner.

6.2 The Forensic Expert's Role

Although the attorneys request the information during the discovery process, they use forensic experts to analyze the information. Forensic experts should carefully read all the information gathered in the discovery process and may wish to focus on material that the retaining attorney expresses. Because the information will be used in court, it is important that they review, evaluate, analyze, and contemplate all the data provided to avoid missing any critical points. Close study of these documents allows the expert to request any additional information needed to more fully express a professional opinion.

Some attorneys, however, provide their experts only with a summary of depositions. This is a potentially dangerous practice because it can inhibit the forensic expert's ability to provide a comprehensive and accurate report and give credible testimony at the deposition or trial. Attorneys usually provide deposition summaries in an effort to save their clients the expense of a forensic expert's evaluation of the full depositions, but this practice contains the risk of influencing the forensic expert, since all pertinent facts may not be provided. Additionally, this exposes the retaining attorney to disclosure of the attorney's work product and may have a negative connotation on cross-examination. The forensic expert should not be shy about determining if there is additional material which would help render an opinion and requesting that information from the attorney.

6.2.1 Getting Complete Information

Forensic experts know much more about the scientific and technical aspects of their respective field than the attorney; therefore, attorneys should not screen sworn testimony. It is the attorney's choice to provide or refrain from providing the forensic expert all requested information. It is the forensic expert's responsibility to ensure the opinions are complete by requesting all needed information.

Since attorneys are not authorities in all fields, forensic experts must be able to convey their opinions and data to attorneys in a way that they can understand and present to the jury. If the attorney does not understand the forensic expert's opinions and report, how will a jury understand the same information and render a reasonable verdict?

6.2.2 Information Management

The forensic expert must devise an efficient system to keep notes and file data. The system can be as simple as a file cabinet with folders or as complex as a comprehensive computer database. The forensic expert should keep all pertinent, relevant, or critical files reviewed, as well as written opinions, notes on discovery reviewed, photos, depositions of opposing experts, and other vital materials. The forensic expert should be able to locate reviewed material quickly and efficiently. It is not uncommon to keep all of the material in a digital form to alleviate space and allow the expert to be able to find the data expediently.

Forensic experts should request a copy of their own deposition transcript. The forensic expert must understand that attorneys can access the forensic expert's prior testimony by contacting court reporters or the attorney who took the prior testimony. Forensic experts should be consistent in their professional opinion and take into account current studies and information if the previous opinions are outdated. Reviewing prior testimony can assure this consistency.

6.2.3 Additional Data Collection

After the discovery process has commenced, it is a good time for the forensic expert to ask the attorney any questions stemming from the review of the discovery materials. Further information may be needed to update opinions. It is also beneficial to ask the attorney how the forensic expert will be formally disclosed to opposing counsel. These questions might require that the forensic expert meet with some of the parties or witnesses involved in the litigation to gather more information. Other forms of additional discovery can include inspections and depositions.

The forensic expert should have all the materials necessary to determine whether additional discovery is needed to render a professional opinion as stated in a disclosure, an affidavit, or a written formal report. It also sheds a positive light on an expert that cares enough about opinions to request additional documentation.

6.3 The Inspection

During the site inspection, the retaining attorney may request the forensic expert to examine the area where the incident occurred, as well as any laboratory results or other physical evidence pertinent to the case. This process gives the forensic expert a firsthand view of the evidence upon which he or she must base an opinion. It is important that this task be accomplished before rendering a formal report or initial opinion.

6.3.1 Inspection Methods

It may be common for the forensic expert to take photos, notes, and measurements during the inspection to ensure all information is accurate and complete regarding the physical environment surrounding any aspect of the case.

The forensic expert should study all previously reviewed documents that could be involved in the inspection. It is the expert's responsibility to bring to the inspection appropriate equipment such as cameras, measuring tapes, and note pads. The forensic expert should allow enough time to gather all necessary information. A good forensic expert who reviews the evidence from both sides may bring out information that can be used to discredit the findings of other experts.

6.3.2 Inspection Restrictions

The attorneys must agree what each side can or cannot do during the inspection. For example, a forensic expert visiting a health club may not be allowed to actually exercise on equipment specifically cited in the litigation. The only access to this equipment might be for photos or measurements, and actual movement of the equipment may be prohibited. This information must be communicated to the forensic expert prior to the inspection, so the expert can prepare an appropriate strategy to gather vital data.

6.3.3 Inspection Etiquette

Many inspections are conducted with forensic experts on both sides present. This may be ordered by the court or agreed to by all the attorneys to facilitate the inspection process and avoid unnecessary inconvenience to personnel at the inspection site. The forensic expert should not, at this time, mention or discuss any specifics regarding the case. While the experts often know each other, they should keep their interaction to a minimum. Communication with the retaining attorney should be done in private. The opposing parties, counsel, or forensic experts should not be able to hear the conversation. A forensic expert who needs additional items or other evidence during the inspection should convey such needs or suggestions to the retaining attorney. It then becomes the responsibility of the attorney to formally request the items or evidence from the opposing attorney. This request is usually verbal, since both attorneys are present.

At this point in the discovery process the forensic expert has thoroughly reviewed all of the information gathered. Now is the time for the expert to communicate to the hiring attorney any additional discovery items that may be needed to draw a professional opinion.

6.4 The Formal Written Report or Affidavit

Although the attorney is responsible for requesting a formal written report, the forensic expert should ask when retained whether a written report will be required and, if so, when it is due. The forensic expert should already be formulating the opinions regardless of whether a report is requested.

6.4.1 Using Notes

Using an organized note-taking system during the investigation of the evidence can go a long way in helping to prepare a report if that is the preference of the forensic expert and retaining attorney. The forensic expert should be aware that notes may be discoverable to the adverse party. If the expert mandates note-taking, it should be conveyed to the retaining attorney who can then make an informed decision as to whether to retain the expert or hire someone else.

6.4.2 Reviewing All Data

Before writing the report, the forensic expert should compile all the data gathered during discovery and review these to determine how the report should be organized. If a report is not requested, the forensic expert should compile all of the data regardless in formulating opinions and review the data before any testimony.

6.4.3 Writing the Report

The expert should write the report only after the attorney has requested it. The forensic expert should clearly state the expert's opinions. The attorney should indicate to the expert the facts required to develop the burden of proof, including state requirements (tests, procedures, diagnoses, etc.). If the forensic expert provides a draft copy for the attorney to review, the expert needs to understand that any draft may be discoverable depending on the jurisdictional rules. Some attorneys request to review drafts before an expert's opinion is finalized and there should be a mutual agreement between the forensic expert and retaining attorney before beginning to draft a report. If the forensic expert allows the retaining attorney to draft the report, the expert must be comfortable that the report accurately reflects the opinions before agreeing to the report's disclosure.

6.4.4 Goals of the Written Report

The retaining attorney must know and understand what the expert witness will say during the trial, and the expert must understand how the attorney will use that testimony. Discovery allows the adverse attorney to determine what the forensic expert will opine at the time of trial. This assists the attorneys in having informed discussions with their clients.

The forensic expert's report should be concise and must be based on testimony and research data from the industry or specific discipline.

In addition, the forensic expert's report should

- State up front whether the report is preliminary or final.
- Identify the formal, educational, and practical experiences, as well as the information discovered in data collection, that helped form the basis for the opinion.
- Refer to specific testimony, documents, and objects as reviewed to provide evidence for the opinions and conclusions expressed in the report.

6.4.5 Maintaining Credibility

An attorney will often suggest alternative ways for the expert to express a conclusion or opinion; however, such suggestions should be limited to elements of style and should not affect the content of the opinion. If the expert believes the retaining attorney is not allowing for an accurate disclosure of opinions, the expert should seek to be removed as a forensic expert in a professional manner.

6.5 Reading the Subpoena

The forensic expert must read the subpoena to find out what specific information will be required at the time of the deposition. A subpoena duces tecum requires production of documents or other tangible items. A subpoena for appearance may be required for appearance at a deposition or trial and must specify a time and location.

7

THE FORENSIC EXPERT'S DEPOSITION

7.1 Preparing for the Deposition

7.1.1 Timing of the Deposition

Once the forensic expert's opinions are disclosed to the adverse party, the opposing counsel may request a deposition of the expert. This does not always happen since settlement hearings and procedures are being carried on at this time as well. Attorneys determine whether the cost of the deposition renders taking the deposition feasible.

Upon notice that the expert is to be deposed, the retaining attorney must explain the significance of the deposition testimony. This is also a good time to fully discuss the various specifics of the deposition. The time, date, and location should be in writing.

7.1.2 Purpose of the Deposition

Depositions serve a number of purposes for both sides. Depositions might be conducted to

- Discover facts, opinions, theories, documents, research
- Meet forensic experts in person—sizing up the opposition
- Discuss and preserve evidence for trial
- Review any trial themes or strategies
- Determine information that can be used at trial for impeachment
- Intimidate the expert
- Provide a basis or incentive for settlement
- Draw out the legal process and its associated costs and fees

In addition, testimony taken during discovery can be utilized in motions prior to trial to assist the judge in determining which claims, defenses, and evidence will be admitted to the jury.

The forensic expert should also keep in mind that the opposing attorney may choose not to depose the expert. Cost may be a reason and the opposing attorney may have a strategic motive to not disclose all of the cross-examination knowledge should the case be more suitable to go to trial.

7.1.3 Communicating with the Attorney

7.1.3.1 Litigation Issues Once all the mechanics of setting up the deposition have been completed, the retaining attorney should communicate with the forensic expert on issues and concerns surrounding the litigation, including the technical and scholarly aspects of the litigation relevant to the deposition testimony. For this communication to be effective and productive, the forensic expert should

- review the discovery data again;
- be thoroughly familiar with specific facts such as names, places, and times; and
- bring all files to be produced by agreement or subpoena duces tecum to the meeting.

This is the opportunity for both the forensic expert and the attorney to express their professional beliefs regarding the direction of the litigation. This is also a good time for the attorney preparing the forensic expert to find out if the expert has done the work required to render a professional opinion. In addition, the forensic expert can ensure that the attorney understands the professional, ethical, and technical position of the expert. The forensic expert needs to be cognizant that any conversation with the attorney is probably discoverable by the adverse party.

The forensic expert should also explain to the retaining attorney what pieces of evidence will be required to assist the expert explain opinions. Evidence comes in two forms, demonstrative and substantive. Substantive evidence is used to prove a fact at issue in the case. Demonstrative evidence does not get admitted into evidence but can be utilized to assist explaining to the adverse attorney, judge, and jury.

7.1.3.2 What to Expect at the Deposition The retaining attorney can explain what can be expected. For example, the attorney can point out key areas upon which the opposing counsel will confront, concentrate on, or criticize in questioning.

Opposing counsel tactics can include

- Attempting to discredit the witness as not being an expert
- Painting the forensic expert as a hired gun rather than an impartial professional rendering an opinion, although this would be counterproductive at a deposition as opposed to testimony at trial
- Attacking the level of knowledge or skill of the forensic expert as not appropriate or substandard
- Accusing the expert of accepting the case at the last minute and rendering an opinion favorable to the hiring attorney's case without fully investigating the facts
- Attacking the fee structure of the forensic expert as excessive or unreasonable
- Questioning the materials the forensic expert used when formulating opinions or conclusions

The forensic expert should ask the question: "What should I expect from the opposing counsel?" The expert must have a clear understanding of the intensity of the upcoming examination. The retaining attorney should make every effort to ensure that the forensic expert has a reasonable expectation of what could happen at the deposition. The retaining attorney may wish to play devil's advocate when preparing the expert for deposition, painting the issues as viewed by the opposing attorney. The forensic expert should be prepared for a stressful and intellectually challenging experience.

The forensic expert should be aware that the adverse attorney taking the deposition may ask about any documents which have been reviewed. The adverse attorney will likely inquire about communications with the retaining attorney including, but not limited to, the predeposition meeting. The expert should communicate in an honest manner without being defensive.

The forensic expert should discuss the role expected at the deposition. Most attorneys want the forensic expert to answer the questions asked without elucidating during the deposition because the time to educate is at the trial and not at the deposition. However, the attorney may recognize that the case is more likely to settle should the adverse party understand the opinions more fully. The forensic expert and retaining attorney need to be on the same page as to what is expected and the forensic expert needs to be able to rely on the retaining attorney to expound on any opinions that need more disclosure during the deposition.

7.1.4 The Role of the Subpoena Duces Tecum

The subpoena duces tecum may illustrate what specific information will be discussed at the time of the deposition. The adverse attorney may discuss the material or choose to ask questions knowing that those documents have been produced and move into different areas of analysis.

7.1.5 The Practice Session

The forensic expert may request time just prior to the deposition for a practice session with the retaining attorney. This time should be spent testing the expert's responses to the questions. It is best for an inexperienced forensic expert to have this meeting in person if possible rather than by phone. Since many forensic experts must travel long distances and such sessions are not always possible, it may be wise to consider scheduling an earlier flight or arriving the night before the deposition if one has to travel. This allows time to relax, meet with the retaining attorney, and discuss deposition strategies and not feel rushed, which could lead to poor testimony.

Experts in any field want to be respected for their work, degrees, and careers; however, opposing counsel may attempt to discredit the forensic expert in a deposition. This strategy is designed to impugn the testimony and impede the performance of the expert. An expert who knows the purpose and understands the process of the deposition will be more capable of coping with and containing this anxiety and should not show any defensiveness.

A coolheaded forensic expert can be of great value to the hiring attorney and a major detriment to the opposition. The key to forensic expert testimony is to respond accurately to the questions asked. The forensic expert should answer only the questions asked and must rely that the retaining expert will ask questions needed should more information need to be disclosed.

7.1.6 The Forensic Expert's Files

The forensic expert is now at the point in the litigation process where his or her work is made under oath. The expert should meet with the retaining attorney before entering the deposition, and share the contents of the expert's complete files on the matter. A general axiom is that any material reviewed in preparation for a deposition, even if privileged, may be discoverable because it was reviewed. It is important to discuss what material to review with the retaining attorney so that there are no surprises at the deposition. Should the attorney request the expert to *lose* a document, it should send up a red flag to the forensic expert and the expert may wish to withdraw from the matter in a professional manner.

7.2 The Deposition

The deposition is a sworn testimony provided under oath. The expert's testimony may be critical to the case and should be conducted with honesty, integrity, and professionalism.

The deposition involves taking the sworn testimony of any and all potential witnesses, experts, and parties involved in the litigation. Depositions are usually held in an attorney's office, but they can be held in any place that is mutually agreed upon by all attorneys. The attorney requesting the deposition can save money by holding the deposition at the expert's office, eliminating the expert's travel fee. The purpose, emotion, and effect of the actual deposition will be examined in detail in this section.

7.2.1 The Nature of the Testimony

The deposition is taken in the presence of all parties and their attorneys, the witness, and a court reporter. The opposing attorney's forensic expert can also be present if the parties agree or if the jurisdiction allows this practice. The opposition may use their forensic expert for intimidation or to help formulate questions.

7.2.1.1 Questions regarding Fees There may be questions concerning the forensic expert's academic or professional experiences as well as fee structure. However, this may not be the case if the attorney has deposed the forensic expert in the past or if that attorney is attempting to catch the forensic expert off guard.

The forensic expert must be satisfied with the payment arrangements or the deposition may be in jeopardy. If the forensic expert is under a subpoena, and is dissatisfied with said payment arrangements, it is recommended that the matter be brought to the attention of the court for resolution.

7.2.1.2 Use of Intimidation Attorneys can ask just about anything they want to within reason but some of the most common tactics used to intimidate the forensic expert include the following:

- Asking the forensic expert a series of questions meant to purposely omit facts in evidence—This is an attempt to get the expert to admit or concede a different opinion or conclusion.
- Presenting a series of hypothetical situations to the forensic expert and demanding an opinion or conclusion—These situations are usually designed to elicit opinions or conclusions that would be different from those previously rendered.
- Badgering the forensic expert or being threatening or condescending—Posing misleading questions or presenting details of little real value to confuse the forensic expert about the facts as being presented.
- Asking the forensic expert to list items or actions taken to render their opinions—This is designed to box the forensic expert into a simple *no* answer to the final question of the attorney taking the deposition: "Is there anything else to this list?" This *no* answer can limit the expert in later testimony or force the expert to clarify the answer. The opposing counsel uses such situations to make the forensic expert appear either incompetent or dishonest.

Forensic experts should be cognizant to render accurate opinions and should not feel forced into rendering any inaccurate opinions because of intimidation. Good attorneys know how to patronize or bully experts into producing opinions, which can be devastating to the client's case. The expert may want to indicate that the attorney is making the expert uncomfortable. If asked a hypothetical, the forensic expert may want to clarify that "based on the hypothetical with the limited facts provided, the opinion is as follows. ..." Remember, the deposition testimony will be used at trial to impeach the forensic expert.

7.2.1.3 Use of Objections At times during the deposition, the retaining attorney may object, on the record, to specific questions or statements made by the opposing counsel. The expert should not be intimidated by these formal, legal objections. They are part of the legal process and deal with matters not in the professional expertise of the forensic expert. Remember, wait and say nothing during an objection. Let the attorneys battle the legal issues surrounding the objection and wait to be asked the next question.

The two most common objections are *form* and *foundation*. A form objection means the attorney thinks the question is ambiguous or incomplete. Unless instructed otherwise, the forensic expert should answer the question if the expert understands it. A foundation objection means the attorney believes the forensic expert does not have enough information or the question is out of the scope for this expert. Again, the forensic expert can respond unless instructed not to. Sometimes attorneys object simply to be obstreperous or change the mood or cadence of the deposition.

7.2.2 Answering Questions

7.2.2.1 Listen Carefully The forensic expert must be a good listener, as well as a competent speaker. Questions must be answered directly. If the expert does not understand a question or if the question is too compound to respond, the expert should simply ask that the question be restated in a different way. The forensic expert is in charge of expert opinions and needs to feel comfortable with the question before submitting a response.

7.2.2.2 Think before Answering It is acceptable to take a moment to formulate and articulate the best answer. In fact, it is preferable to reflect on the actual question asked before submitting a response. Rambling answers may provide more information than is requested, giving the opposing counsel information for additional examination. It is the job of the attorney taking the deposition to ask the questions. If the attorney has done his or her homework, the right questions will be asked. Never volunteer information unless the retaining attorney asks you to do so.

7.2.2.3 Speak Slowly   As a speaker, the forensic expert must learn to talk slowly, since the court reporter must be able to record every word. The responses must be articulate and professional. Practice answers and review how responses will be structured. Remember, the court reporter cannot take down nods of the head, affirmative gestures, or negative gestures. The response must be verbal and an expert who propounds nonverbal responses appears to be a novice.

7.2.2.4 Correct Mistakes   Do not panic if you make a mistake or miscalculation. If you recognize that a mistake was made during the deposition, ask politely to correct the previous response. If you notice a mistake when reviewing the transcript, utilize the correction page and explain the reason for the modification.

7.2.2.5 Remain Alert and Focused   Pay attention to what is being asked, not how it was asked. Some attorneys try to lull forensic experts into a friendly atmosphere of complacency and then quietly go in for the kill. Some attorneys are aggressive by nature or utilize bullying tactics. No matter what style of questioning the attorney chooses, remain calm, respectful, and focused. You are the expert and are not on trial. Do not take the deposition as a personal attack on your career or credibility.

Do not lose focus. Stay with your conclusions unless given evidence previously not disclosed that could cause a change. It may be best to consult the retaining attorney in private before proceeding with an answer if that is allowed in the jurisdiction.

7.2.2.6 Stay within Your Area of Expertise   The forensic expert must never stray from his or her expertise or defend a qualification where none exists. The attorney who retained the expert should have very carefully examined the forensic expert's areas of expertise. If asked a question that takes the forensic expert out of his or her field of expertise, the expert is obligated to say, "I cannot answer that question since it's not within my area of expertise." Experts that go beyond their scope of expertise can create major problems for themselves and the retaining client. The overreaching expert will be exposed to being stricken as an expert or minimally discredited as an expert in any field. Additionally, attorneys utilizing the Internet and Listservs will undoubtedly learn of the expert's overreaching and it will become harder to get hired and easier to cross-examine the forensic expert in the future.

Remember, in depositions, the purpose is to ascertain the professional opinions of the forensic expert as well as to size up how he or she may appear on the stand at trial. An expert who is overextending is easier to attack at trial.

7.2.2.7 Express Opinions Clearly One area that can cause both confusion and problems for a jury is the difference between *possibility*, *probability*, and *certainty* when expressing an opinion. Juries may be instructed to consider only those opinions that are expressed to a "reasonable degree of probability." Therefore, the forensic expert must be careful when asked to render a possibility opinion. The term *probability* refers to over 50%, while *possibility* is fewer than 50%. Some jurisdictions use *certainty* in the same manner as *probability*, although the term *certainty* has a much stronger connotation.

7.2.2.8 Tell the Truth Perjury is never an option. Giving false statements under oath—either in deposition or at trial—to cover up or misrepresent evidence is a crime and could likely prohibit the forensic expert from being retained in the future. The court can impose sanctions including fines and potential loss of liberty.

7.2.3 The Forensic Expert's Opinions

Forensic experts who express opinions must be able and ready to lay a proper foundation as to how the opinion was derived. This foundation is the professional experience, academic background, and review of all the evidence. This information should be found in the written report or affidavit, if generated, and if requested by the retaining attorney. The deposition is the place in the litigation process where the forensic expert and the retaining attorney can begin to see how the complexities of the case will be presented. The stronger the forensic expert's foundation, the more likely the opposing attorney may want to encourage a settlement prior to trial.

When expressing a scientific foundation, forensic experts must be careful about using scientific evidence that has not been validated by the mainstream professional community or applicable industry. This is known as *junk science*. This includes theories that have been set forth to examine and explain some results, but that have not been researched or accepted by the learned societies of the forensic expert's colleagues.

7.3 Conclusion of the Deposition

The court stenographer reports only verbal cues and may spell unfamiliar words incorrectly. Therefore, spend a few moments with the court reporter following the deposition to make sure names, places, or technical information is correctly spelled since most court reporters will highlight these for review.

At the end of the deposition, the expert may be requested to read the transcript and make corrections or waive the review process. The forensic expert should discuss this with the retaining attorney before the deposition and determine who would pay for the review. It is generally a good idea for the forensic expert to review and make corrections; however, the expert must be careful to actually review and make needed corrections within the time provided. Any corrections can be discussed with the jury as well as the initial answer to the expert should be especially careful in the deposition to answer the questions asked as best as possible.

Once the deposition is concluded, the forensic expert may want to meet with the retaining attorney for feedback. The attorney should be clear and precise as to how he or she perceived the testimony of the forensic expert and how a judge or jury may perceive such testimony. This feedback can be quite valuable to forensic experts as they continue their consulting, and in future testimony situations.

7.4 After the Deposition

7.4.1 Review of the Deposition

Upon completion of the deposition, the forensic expert has the opportunity to ask on the record to review the deposition, make corrections, and sign it. If the expert reserves this opportunity, it is returned to the court reporter. In some states, the original transcript is sealed and kept by the attorney taking the deposition. This original is not opened until the trial.

Forensic experts should take the time to carefully read their testimony as presented in the deposition. Any changes should be made on the forms that are attached to their copy. It is a good practice to inform the retaining attorney of any substantive changes; however, most corrections are minor or grammatical.

Forensic experts should keep a copy of their depositions since they may be required to reveal their stated opinions in future testimony.

7.4.2 Status Check

The forensic expert should ask the hiring attorney about the status of the case and what other consulting tasks may be requested.

Tasks and questions may include the following:

- Reviewing additional testimony.
- Reviewing new discovery items.
- A timeline as to the expert's future involvement in the litigation—This can involve supplemental written reports or other statements (affidavits) needed to answer various motions made by opposing counsel. Some of these motions can include a motion for summary judgment and or a motion in limine.
- Anticipating other motions anticipated on either side.

7.4.3 Additional Information

The opinions of the expert may change due to the review of new information provided after the deposition. If this situation were to occur, the forensic experts must communicate the change immediately to the retaining attorney.

The forensic experts should never hesitate to ask the retaining attorney for further information from other people who should be deposed or additional discovery that may be needed. However, it is the attorney's decision as to what additional discovery is appropriate for the forensic expert to review at this point in the litigation. Since the forensic expert has been reviewing more data, there should be ongoing billing to the retaining attorney.

7.4.4 Settlement Negotiations

Settlement is the most common resolution to many disputes. During the settlement hearings or discussions, both parties attempt to resolve their differences. Money is usually the point of contention during these negotiations, which may include the cost of forensic experts.

Should the parties involved not reach a settlement, however, the litigation proceeds to trial. Any case can be settled at any time up to and through trial.

8
The Trial

8.1 The Role of the Forensic Expert in the Trial Strategy

Forensic experts are often the key to trial strategy. Only the forensic expert can testify with any credibility on technical issues and standards of care. Although opinions on the technical aspects of the litigation are the responsibility of the forensic expert, the expert may assist in the theme of the trial. The attorney needs to know how the forensic expert feels about the issues as well as how facts and evidence should be presented.

8.2 Preparing for Trial

8.2.1 Attorney–Expert Communication

The attorney must develop questions for all witnesses at trial. These questions should accurately reflect the theme and the strategy as they relate to the forensic expert's portions of the testimony. This is a perfect time for the attorney and the forensic expert to meet and share mutual concerns and suggestions as to the direct examination of the forensic expert at trial.

The attorney has to determine whether the forensic expert will represent his or her professional opinions at trial in a manner that will advance the theme and the strategy as devised. The forensic expert must feel comfortable and competent to render professional opinions. Without this level of competence, the forensic expert can appear weak and unconvincing at trial.

Remember, the testimony of any forensic expert must never be contingent upon the outcome of the trial. This is a matter of law in some states but should always be a matter of ethics for all forensic experts.

8.2.2 Preparing Technical Information and Exhibits

Forensic experts must be clear as to what exhibits they wish to use during their testimony. The attorney must be confident that the forensic expert can professionally and vigorously provide the foundation for the exhibit to be entered into evidence. The forensic expert needs to meet with the attorney to learn exactly what forms of exhibits are to be used in court. The forensic expert may also wish to utilize demonstrative exhibits which are useful in explaining opinions but are not actually admitted into evidence.

The forensic expert must always be aware of any and all exhibits that will be used at trial during his or her testimony. The forensic expert cannot typically expect the attorney to present an exhibit that the forensic expert first provided at the day of trial. The communication between the forensic expert and the attorney must be crystal clear on these points before trial testimony. The forensic experts should have a consulting role in the development of all the exhibits that pertain to their testimony from the inception of the case. Failure to be knowledgeable about such exhibits could result in the testimony being confusing to the jury.

The forensic expert must formulate how to present technical information to a lay jury. This approach must be communicated to the attorney so that just the right amount of technical information is given with an appropriate nontechnical explanation.

8.2.3 Preparing for Testimony

To best prepare for their expert testimony, forensic experts should review all notes and any other documents they have used as bases for their professional opinions. This may increase the costs but is necessary for the forensic experts to present their opinions with credibility and factual data. Along with a review of all the documents mentioned, forensic experts must review their own deposition. This review is critical since experts must avoid stating anything on the stand that could be interpreted as contradictory to their previous testimony at deposition. This is also a good review of the issues surrounding the litigation, since the forensic experts provided their foundation and opinions at the deposition.

Before the trial, attorneys and forensic experts must reflect and examine the deposition testimony regarding specific areas of testimony that may become potential problems at the trial.

It is important for the expert to review with the retaining attorney some of the key questions the counsel should ask the expert on the stand. Attorneys may forget or state a question in such a way that is different from the approach taken in earlier discussions with the forensic expert, so the expert needs to listen carefully on the stand.

The forensic expert also needs to communicate any weaknesses in their opinions, conclusions, or foundations, so that the retaining attorney and the expert avoid being viewed as attempting to hide or obfuscate the facts. The opposing counsel has a good chance of bringing out the facts during cross-examination anyway, so it may be best to dispose of these issues during direct examination.

By far the most stressful activity for a forensic expert is the testimony on the witness stand. Only with continued and open communications between the forensic expert and the attorney can this part of the litigation process be completed with dignity and effectiveness.

8.2.4 Billing before Trial

Forensic experts should provide their hiring attorney with a complete billing for all professional consulting services rendered at the time.

8.2.5 The Trial Subpoena

The forensic expert can but generally does not have to request a subpoena. The subpoena is the formal request by the court to appear at trial. Most attorneys will serve a subpoena to their witnesses and will want to confirm whether their experts require one. Theoretically, a subpoena ensures that the witness will appear in court.

8.3 The Trial Process

All of the parties are present in the courtroom. There are typically various motions and other legal matters being brought up to the judge by the legal counsel representing these parties.

8.3.1 Jury Selection

Once all motions and legal matters are resolved, the jury panel is assembled in the courtroom and the judge addresses them. The bailiff then calls, at random, names of jury members to be brought into the jury box.

8.3.1.1 The Judge Questions Potential Jurors   The judge will typically question each juror as to basic facts such as marriage, occupation, children, and previous experiences as a juror or party. Attorneys submit a list of questions called *voir dire* that either they wish the judge to ask or they want to ask depending on the preference of the court.

8.3.1.2 The Attorneys Question Potential Jurors—Voir Dire   Attorneys may have the opportunity to further question each potential juror depending on the court. The duration of voir dire depends on the judge, the jurisdiction, and the nature of the action.

8.3.1.3 The Attorneys Challenge Potential Jurors   Each party has unlimited challenges for cause. These challenges may be automatic, such as when a potential juror is related to one of the parties involved in the lawsuit. Other challenges for cause can be elicited through statements made by a potential juror, for example, statements of potential jurors admitting that they cannot be fair and impartial. Most attorneys have found that the majority of people will not admit publicly that they are prejudiced or biased. Therefore, the attorney must formulate questions designed to bring such feelings and values before the court.

Once the reasons for this challenge are given, the opposing attorney has the opportunity to object to the challenge. The judge then will rule on the matter. This open questioning of a juror is sometimes more problematic for the attorney invoking the challenge, since this juror now may develop a dislike for that attorney. Therefore, challenges for cause are usually handled in private; however, other judges may want the entire jury to be present during this time.

After the attorneys make their challenges for cause, they have the opportunity to strike a certain number of panel members.

Parties are usually of the belief that they get a "jury of their peers"; however, the reality is that the remaining panel members constituting the jury are usually people that were so average that neither party felt they were a threat. Attorneys and parties are not allowed to strike jurors for protected reasons such as race, national origin, and sex.

8.3.1.4 The Jury Is Selected Once this process is completed, the list of jury members is given to the judge and the names of the people selected to serve on the jury are announced. To many legal experts, this is one of the two times in the trial process when a case is won or lost.

8.3.2 Opening Statements

Plaintiffs or prosecutors go first. They have the burden of proof and typically occupy the counsel table closest to the jury. The attorneys usually tell the jury what they believe the evidence will prove in the litigation. While the attorneys will attempt to state facts during this opening statement by describing what witnesses and exhibits will be presented, they are presenting, in essence, their theory or theme. This first impression is critical, since it can provide a framework upon which the jury may base their impressions of testimony, evidence, and arguments presented during the trial.

8.3.3 Giving Testimony

Courtroom testimony is the aspect of forensic experts' work that illustrates their research and professionalism. This is about the ultimate goal for forensic experts. It is during this time that forensic experts must present themselves as authorities in their respective fields and win the respect of the jury as a professional whose opinions will become part of the basis for their verdict. Therefore, it is critical that the forensic expert arrives on time and in top form, ready to shine as a professional.

8.3.3.1 Arrive Early The forensic expert should be at the court at least 15 minutes before the scheduled testimony. The forensic expert must understand that very often the time given to appear at trial may be vastly different from the actual time of testimony, since the court's timetable may change due to unforeseen issues.

Delays are common. Be sure to set aside adequate time to accommodate such delays. Forensic experts must realize that their testimony is only one part of the entire trial. Attorneys try to schedule experts as best they can, but they often miscalculate the time required to question other witnesses.

8.3.3.2 Expect to Stay The forensic expert should generally plan to be at court longer than common sense dictates. Otherwise, the expert's testimony may be affected by frustration or concern about missed appointments or flights home.

8.3.3.3 Enter the Courtroom Appropriately The forensic expert should refrain from entering the courtroom during proceedings without being called unless specifically directed to do so by the retaining attorney. Most courtrooms have a sign on the door indicating the rules concerning the exclusion of witnesses from the courtroom. Should the forensic expert appear in the courtroom without being called, the judge may halt the proceedings and request the expert to leave. Although not a major problem in most cases, this situation can be embarrassing to the forensic expert and may affect the jury's impression when that expert testifies.

8.3.3.4 Dress Appropriately Dress professionally neat, but also dress according to the local customs. There may be special conditions imposed by the judge as to the atmosphere of the court.

Ask the attorney to discuss how he or she wants you to appear in terms of dress. The retaining attorney should have a clear expectation of what the expert should wear, so it is important to receive that input.

8.3.3.5 Know What to Expect Ask the retaining attorney about the cultural environment of the courtroom, as well as the judge's style and operation of the courtroom. The attorney may inform the forensic expert of any previous experiences with the judge. This can include how the judge conducts the court proceedings and what specific rules are to be followed by all forensic experts who appear in that courtroom.

8.3.3.6 Show Respect   Never leave the witness stand unless asked to by the attorney or the judge, and never approach the jury unless permission is granted. Never speak when the judge interrupts the proceedings. Wait until the judge or the attorney instructs the forensic expert to continue testimony. There are likely to be many objections during the proceedings and you need to be prepared for them. Do not use or have your cell phone with you.

8.3.4 Direct Examination of the Forensic Expert

The retaining attorney questions the forensic expert first during direct examination. The direct attorney usually attempts to introduce evidence, opinions, and conclusions favorable to the client's case, and the atmosphere is usually respectful and congenial.

The testimony of the forensic expert can be made more effective when the communication between the attorney and the forensic expert is conducted in a systematic manner. The questions posed by the attorney must be clear to the forensic expert. In responding to those questions, the forensic expert should be confident, professional, concise, and skilled in explaining opinions in a fashion that the jury can comprehend.

The forensic expert should be able and willing to render a professional opinion, based on sound academic, practical, or researched foundations.

8.3.5 Cross-Examination of the Forensic Expert

Following direct examination by the retaining attorney, the opposing counsel will have an opportunity to cross-examine the expert.

The forensic expert should discuss the probable tactics of the adverse attorney for cross-examination. The attorney may share with the expert any perceived weaknesses in the theme or the strategy of the case on the part of either the attorney or the forensic expert.

It is a mistake for a forensic expert to fail to prepare for the cross-examination. The expert should be congenial and direct in all responses. Again, just answer the questions with integrity, honesty, and professional ethics. If the expert feels that the answer cannot be made with just a yes or no, the expert should respectfully state, "I cannot answer that question with just a yes or no; would you like me to explain why?" This may pose a problem for the cross-examining attorney who would appear to be obviating the facts if the answer is no. If the cross-examining attorney responds affirmatively, it lets the jury know that the expert is in control and allows the expert to educate the jury about the opinions.

8.3.6 The Redirect of the Forensic Expert

Some courts allow for a redirect, while other judges are reticent. Redirect examination is supposed to be utilized only for discussing and elaborating on responses given during the cross-examination.

8.3.7 The Directed Verdict

At the close of the presenting party's case, the adverse side may request a directed verdict. The directed verdict is an attempt to have the court rule as a matter of law that the adverse side did not prove its case or defense. In a civil case, the burden of proof is generally by a preponderance of the evidence, which means greater than 50%. The burden of proof in some civil claims, usually involving punitive damages, is "clear and convincing." In criminal cases, the burden of proof is "beyond a reasonable doubt."

8.3.8 The Defense Presents Its Case

The defense will call its own witnesses and forensic experts and introduce its own exhibits. The defense forensic experts are now subject to cross-examination by the plaintiff's or prosecuting attorney.

The strategy of the defense will be to portray the same issues in a light that is favorable to its position. The old adage "There are two sides to every story" is clear at this time in the trial proceedings. If there were not two sides to every story, we would not have a need for trials.

Obviously, the defense forensic experts must meet the same high level of performance and professionalism as the plaintiff's forensic experts.

However, the discussions surrounding the same review of documents and their opinions or conclusions may be different. Additionally, their opinions may not deal with the same documents. For example, one forensic expert may pay attention to items different from those in the case of the opposing forensic expert.

If the plaintiff's or prosecuting attorney does not believe that the defense has proven its case to the burden of proof, he or she may ask for a directed verdict. Again, this is a request that the judge rules as a matter of law that the defense was inadequate so that the jury cannot consider it.

8.3.9 Jury Instructions

Once the defense has rested, the judge will present the instructions to the jury. Attorneys for all parties will have submitted their suggested jury instructions to the court. This discussion usually occurs in the judge's chambers or outside the presence of the jurors. Many times these discussions are held after hours or during breaks.

The court attempts to maximize regular working hours for jury convenience, as opposed to having the jury wait for hours while these types of activities are being resolved. Forensic experts need to recognize that the expert is on the stand for only a short duration compared to the significant amount of time that the members of the jury contribute to the process.

The court system in our country is generous with all parties. Everyone has a right to be heard and each case is handled individually. The forensic expert must realize this aspect of the court system and be aware of possible last-minute changes in time frames. Attorneys should communicate these intricacies to their forensic experts to help avoid missed appointments and flights while at trial.

8.3.10 Closing Arguments

Once the defense has rested its case and the jury instructions have been read to the members, the closing arguments begin. The plaintiff or prosecutor presents his or her closing arguments first. This is followed by the defense, which is ultimately followed by the plaintiff or prosecutor again. The plaintiff's counsel or prosecutor gets the last argument because they have the burden of proof.

During these closing arguments, the attorneys will attempt to capsulate their positions using again, in many instances, the testimony of the forensic experts. The attorneys in their closing arguments will most often use a thematic approach. Every attorney has a different style. Some are more emotional, while others are more detail oriented. Regardless of style, this is the last opportunity each side has to present its themes and positions to the jury.

8.3.11 Jury Deliberations

The judge now directs the jury to begin its deliberations. The jury, in most cases, will render a decision that is announced in the courtroom with all parties present. This concludes the trial portion of the litigation.

8.3.12 Post-Trial Motions

Once the verdict is rendered, the attorneys often begin various post-trial motions. For the most part, the forensic expert is not actively involved at this time. Post-trial motions may be followed by appeals to higher courts. A common misconception is that a bad verdict is an automatic appeal. To have a successful appeal, there must be a mistake of law rendered by the court and an adverse verdict is not necessarily a mistake of law.

Occasionally, the forensic expert will be asked to assist the attorney in providing additional feedback, but the evidence is usually on the record. No new evidence can be presented on appeal since the court will consider only the evidence presented at the trial.

8.4 After the Trial

8.4.1 Obtaining Feedback

8.4.1.1 Jury Feedback   It is common practice for attorneys to seek feedback from the jurors as to their opinions and the specific factors they considered when rendering their verdict. Sometimes jurors are willing to provide feedback and sometimes they are not. Feedback is useful for attorneys as they attempt to study their demeanor and behavior after trials. Attorneys also want information on how the evidence, facts, eyewitnesses, exhibits, and forensic experts were perceived.

Forensic experts should inquire into this feedback to learn how they were perceived at trial. This is a learning lesson for future forensic work.

8.4.1.2 Attorney Feedback The forensic expert should ask the retaining attorney about the testimony as soon as possible. Attorneys may be considering their next case and are quick to forget specific feedback during this postmortem period that would be of great benefit to the forensic expert. This information can help the forensic expert evaluate his or her performance and can provide tips on improving performance the next time.

There will be times when a jury did not appreciate, respect, or believe a forensic expert during testimony. The impact of this situation can most certainly cause problems for the party who has retained that forensic expert. Juries come to conclusions by means that are sometimes hard for the forensic expert, as well as the attorney, to understand. Regardless of this fact of life in the litigation process, it benefits the forensic expert to get this feedback from the attorney, because in the final analysis, the reputation and integrity of the forensic expert is at stake.

8.4.1.3 Client Feedback The forensic expert might want to ask the attorney about his or her client's reaction to the testimony. However, the forensic expert must realize that there were many factors, including the client's testimony, that affected the jury's decision. In fact, the verdict might have little or no relationship to the forensic expert's testimony.

8.4.2 Self-Evaluation and Reflections

By understanding how and why a jury reaches a verdict, both attorneys and their forensic experts can learn and improve their future performance. Failure to undertake this final phase of the litigation process can have a serious impact on the professional careers of both attorneys and forensic experts.

9
Professional Practices

9.1 The Role of Credibility, Reputation, and Professional Discipline in Forensic Consulting

Credibility, reputation, and professional discipline are all tools of the forensic expert's practice. Forensic experts should not present their credentials in any way that could be used to impeach their ability to be recognized by the court and the jury as an expert in their field.

Forensic experts should abstain from embellishing their résumé or rendering an opinion that could be attacked by the opposing counsel as not being academically or professionally sound. An overreaching expert or one who provides opinions beyond the scope of expertise may seriously affect the forensic expert's efficacy to the jury as an honest and truthful witness.

9.1.1 Providing a Scientific Foundation

Forensic experts who express an opinion must be able and ready to lay a proper foundation to illustrate exactly how that opinion was reached. This foundation is the professional, academic, and/or researched study of all the evidence and how that evidence is viewed from the professional's point of view. However, when expressing scientific foundation, forensic experts must be careful about using only scientific evidence that has been validated by the mainstream professional community or applicable industry.

9.1.2 Methods for Rendering Professional Opinions

The forensic expert should be able and willing to render a professional opinion based on sound academic, practical, or researched foundation.

The following suggestions can also assist the forensic expert in rendering testimony at trial.

9.1.2.1 Be Prepared Do your homework on the facts and evidence you have reviewed. Be prepared to answer hypothetical questions. Make sure that you begin your response with "Based upon the hypothetical presented with the facts in the hypothetical…."

9.1.2.2 Be Honest Tell the truth based on your research of the evidence. It is important to note that the forensic expert should not be concerned with whether his or her opinion will hurt or damage the arguments for either side. Perjury is a crime; never knowingly make a false statement.

If you do not know the answer to a question, admit that fact and indicate that you will conduct additional research to develop an accurate response.

9.1.2.3 Speak Clearly and Authoritatively Be able to express your opinions in your own words and educate the jury at a level they can understand. A comfortable level of rapport should be established between the forensic expert and the jury. This should include a relaxed posture, but one of confidence. Speak loudly enough for the jury and the judge to hear you. Attempt to keep eye contact with the jurors as long as you feel that the jurors are willing and the eye contact is not obtrusive.

Avoid getting lost in detail that is not of significant value to the fundamental opinions or conclusions. This type of testimony can waste time on the witness stand and confuse the jury.

Be prepared to answer "yes" or "no." Also, do not be afraid to respond with "I don't know" or "I can't remember." However, not remembering a specific important fact can be detrimental. Remember, it is perjury to state that you do not know something if, in fact, you do know it. Not knowing and not remembering are totally different in the eyes of the legal system.

9.1.2.4 Always Stay Calm Never get defensive, angry, or argumentative on the witness stand. Remember, the forensic expert is there to educate jurors and not to win or lose a case. Maintain your composure with dignity on the stand from the time you enter until the time you exit the courtroom.

9.1.2.5 Do Not Exaggerate   Never embellish or exaggerate your opinions; stay with the level of conviction you know to be reasonable and justifiable from a professional viewpoint.

9.1.2.6 Listen Carefully/Answer Thoughtfully   Develop superb listening skills. The forensic expert needs to take time while on the witness stand. Listen carefully to each question and answer only the question being asked. Wait for each question to be asked and then think before you speak. The converse is also true here. Do not wait too long to respond to a question, since this may indicate a lack of knowledge or that your confidence is weak regarding that portion of your testimony.

9.1.2.7 Do Not Attack Other Experts   Do not attack a fellow forensic expert in a personal manner. It may be appropriate to professionally criticize another forensic expert's opinions, résumé, or preparation, but let the attorney attack the forensic expert as to biases, prejudices, or motives.

9.1.2.8 Be Professional   Always appear serious and avoid jokes or anecdotes unless you have significant experience on the witness stand and attempting such a demonstration is acceptable to the court. Never stray beyond your expertise.

9.1.2.9 Keep Conclusions Probable or to a Certainty   Whenever feasible, avoid the word *possible* on direct examination and use *probability* or *certainty* if that is the key word in that jurisdiction. Make certain that the conclusions are fully supported by the evidence.

9.1.2.10 Be Humble   It is the attorney's role to present the academic or experience background of the forensic expert. However, when asked to present qualifications, present yourself in a humble, honest, and simple manner. Do not overstress qualifications. If they are appropriate, the jury and the judge will recognize them. If you make a statement in error, correct it yourself before it comes up in cross-examination.

9.1.2.11 Be Organized   When presenting testimony that involves the use and introduction of exhibits, be well organized and able to take the jury through these exhibits in a manner that they can clearly understand. If the courtroom is electronic, be prepared to utilize that technology if possible.

9.2 Stipulating Responsibilities to the Attorney

The communication between the attorney and the forensic expert must be honest, complete, and professional at all times. There must be a clear understanding of the different roles and responsibilities of the consulting and forensic expert. The forensic expert discloses potential conflicts of interest properly (philosophical differences of opinion, previous testimony, previous relationships with opposing parties, etc.).

9.3 Sharing Files Appropriately

Comply with subpoenas and subpoenas duces tecum. Make certain that the retaining attorney is aware of the subpoena and let the attorney know whether you have objections. Let the retaining attorney decide whether to file a motion to strike the subpoena, a motion for protective order, or a motion to quash. If the attorney indicates that something should be removed from your file, this should represent a red flag and the expert may wish to professionally withdraw.

9.4 Final Billing

At this point, all interested parties have completed their tasks. The forensic expert needs to submit a final billing as soon as possible for any outstanding professional activities performed. The attorneys are preparing their final costs and statements to their clients and need this information.

9.5 Concluding on a Good Note

Forensic experts should make every effort to communicate their appreciation to the retaining attorney. The goal is to be remembered as a professional and to be recommended to other attorneys. Utilize this time to network and stay in communication with the attorney.

Communication between the attorney and the forensic expert must be honest, complete, and professional at all times during this process. The client has the right to professional legal representation by counsel and that also includes the selection, use, and assistance of the forensic expert.

When all is said and done, it is for the jury and judge to decide the outcome. Do the best job possible with the clear understanding that the result may not be what is hoped for or expected. Skilled forensic experts willing to meet the challenges set before them by the legal system help ensure the ability of the legal system to service clients with dignity and competence.

Additional Sources

http://www.crfc.org/americanjury/voir_dire.html.
http://definitions.uslegal.com/d/discovery-request-for-inspection/.
http://www.law.cornell.edu/wex/deposition.
http://www.lectlaw.com/def/d058.htm.
http://legal-dictionary.thefreedictionary.com/interrogatories.
http://www.techlawjournal.com/glossary/legal/summary.htm.